Living Sufism

Rituals in the Middle East and the Balkans

Nicolaas Biegman

The American University in Cairo Press

Cairo New York

Copyright © 2009 by
The American University in Cairo Press
113 Sharia Kasr el Aini, Cairo, Egypt
420 Fifth Avenue, New York, NY 10018
www.aucpress.com

This edition published by arrangement with KIT Publishers BV

Dar el Kutub No. 16954/08
ISBN 978 977 416 263 3

Dar el Kutub Cataloging-in-Publication Data

Biegman, Nicolaas
        Living Sufism: Photographs of Sufi Rituals in the Middle East and the Balkans / François Burgat; translated
    by Nicolaas Biegman.—Cairo: The American University in Cairo Press, 2008
        p.   cm.
        ISBN 977 416 263 3
        1. Sufism—Middle East   2. Sufism—Balkans   I. Title
        297.4

Graphic design
Studio Agaatsz bNO, Meppel, The Netherlands

Production
High Trade, Zwolle, The Netherlands

Printed in Hungary

We draw closer to God by singing.
You can sing with your voice, or with your body.

Abdul Fattah Qalaaji,
Aleppo, Syria

Contents

Introduction

A Different Islam

This book is about extremists.

There are in this world over a billion Muslims. Though they share a basic creed – "there is no god but God, and Muhammad is His messenger" – their religion contains a number of trends and nuances and lacks a central authority to decide on matters of doctrine: so much so that it is difficult to speak of 'Islam' in a general sense.

It can be said, however, that among Muslims there are two extremes. At one extreme we see the fundamentalist 'Islamists,' whether of the Wahhabi, Salafi, Jihadi or another, similar, persuasion such as the Taliban, who are wedded to their literal interpretation of the holy texts. They are exclusive, politicized, and vociferous. They are convinced of possessing the one true faith and do not exclude violent options in defending and spreading it. Music, dance, and entertainment are taboo, and are prohibited wherever these fundamentalists come to power.

At the other extreme we find the Sufis, the mystics within Islam, who are in love with God. Rather than clinging to the letter, they believe in an inner meaning of texts and rituals. They respect different creeds and

opinions and they abhor violence. Music and rhythmic movement are an essential part of the rituals that allow them to draw closer to God.

Both trends are present in the Sunni as well as the Shi'a sects, the principal branches of Islam.

Especially since September 2001, there has been a tendency in the West to identify Islam in its totality with the fundamentalist extreme and with the excesses, both verbal and tangible, perpetrated by its adherents. Sufism is an integral part of the Islamic tradition and the Sufis are more numerous than the fundamentalists. They are not without influence on modern trends in Islam. Yet they remain largely in the background because of a lack of ambition to rule or proselytize, and mostly because they do not want to cause any trouble. No mess, no press.

There certainly exists an awareness of certain aspects of Sufism in Western Europe and North America. Medieval Sufi poets and thinkers such as Rumi and Ibn Arabi have become best-selling authors there. The whirling dervishes from Turkey perform to general acclaim in Western theaters. Some in the West know about or even belong to the Sufi movement introduced there by Inayat

Khan during the first decades of the last century. The movement was based on Muslim Sufism but incorporated various other elements, as well. Yet the Western public doesn't realize that Sufism continues to inspire and guide millions of Muslims all over the world. Sufism is alive and kicking. As the importance of militant Islamism tends to be overestimated, there is an underestimation of the size and vigor of the mystic trend.

In a number of predominantly Muslim countries the Sufis constitute a silent but massive barrier against fundamentalist propaganda. In some, Sufism has become an integral part of post-modern religiosity. Apart from that, the Sufi tradition comprises an important cultural component, especially in music and poetry – much of classical Persian poetry is Sufi – and an attitudinal one that embraces modesty, sincerity, patience, and hospitality. Their ritual, inspired by love of the Divine, can reach spectacular levels of passion.

The ritual and the music are what attracted me in the first place when I stumbled upon present-day Sufism in 1965. It was a summer evening. High above a narrow street somewhere behind the mosque of Al-Husayn in the old city of Cairo there were light bulbs on a string. In the street there was a platform with three musicians and a singer. Their songs, obviously of a religious character, had a penetrating rhythm. A few dozen men were dancing vigorously to the music. I had no idea what all of it meant. Nothing in seven years of study of Arabic, Turkish, and Islam at the University of Leiden had pre-

pared me for the discovery of this enchanted world, with which I fell in love at first sight.

Someone gave me a glass of tea and explained that this was a zikr, a ritual performed by Sufis to increase their nearness to God. They were also celebrating the birthday, the moulid, of a saint.

It was easy to find out about other festivities such as this one. There were always people around who knew when and where I could attend another moulid. Apart from that, most Sufi groups held sessions once or twice a week without any specific occasion.

In the course of two extended stays in Egypt in the 1960s and 1980s, seven years in all, I found that most Sufis didn't object to the presence of a respectful outsider, even when he was using a camera. Some of their sheikhs were willing and able to explain the meaning and background of the rituals. This launched me on a voyage of discovery in various corners of Cairo and Egypt, which ended with the publication of a book with over one hundred photos of saints' festivals: *Egypt: Moulids, Saints, Sufis*, which appeared in English and Dutch versions in 1990 and recently also in Arabic. It did contain some photos of the zikr, but most of the material was to do with the fun, games, trade, and folklore connected with the birthday celebrations for the saints.

With time, it became clear that Sufis in other countries were as willing to welcome a visitor as their Egyptian brothers had been. This made me think I might attempt a photo book focused on Sufi ritual, which had been described but – with the exception of the whirling dervishes – seldom visually shown in any publication. A two-year period in Macedonia gave me the opportunity to test this idea. The outcome was positive. *God's Lovers*, about a Sufi community with an ecstatic ritual, which I befriended in Skopje, came out in 2007 as a first installment.

There are millions of Sufis all over the Muslim world, organized in a plethora of autonomous communities, each with their own customs and traditions. It was out of the question to even think of compiling an overview of their rituals. I therefore decided to concentrate on the two regions I knew best, the Balkans and the Middle East, and there to select a few countries where I had lived or traveled and where I could make myself understood in the local language. Within those countries I looked for a small number of groups who, taken together, would give an approximately accurate impression of Sufi ritual as a whole, with its enormous variety in discipline and exuberance, intellectualism and spontaneity.

Thus, I returned to Egypt and the Rifa'i dervishes of Sheikh Zahir, whom I had known since the 1980s. I also went back to Macedonia, where I knew a Sufi community whose ceremonies differed in many ways from the ones portrayed in *God's Lovers*. I had become familiar with Kosovo during numerous visits out of Skopje, and visited the Rifa'is in Rahovec/Orahovac. Bosnia and Herzegovina could be covered by car from my summer home in Croatia, and turned out to possess a proud Sufi tradition.

Aside from the Syrian Rifa'is, with their exceptional rituals – who just happened to cross my path – the Sufis mentioned in this book belong to orders that are relatively numerous or even preponderant in their respective countries. Within this variety the Egyptian dervishes shown in Chapter Four find themselves somewhere in the middle between the sobriety of the 'sitting' orders and the exotic practices of those with an 'iron faith'.

This is first and foremost a photo book. I have tried to limit the text to what would help the reader understand what is happening in the photographs, and I have relied as much as possible on what those involved in these happenings had to say.

No one was more involved than Sheikh Zahir, my Egyptian friend and informant of over twenty years. I have always admired the Sheikh for his ability to explain in simple terms the intricacies of Sufism, with its central notions of love, light, and the heart. He gave me an extensive interview, in which he draws examples from sports and driving, compares contact with God to the use of a mobile telephone, and unwittingly echoes Yogi Berra's maxim: "If the world were perfect, it wouldn't be." The interview is reproduced in Chapter Three.

Should I be accused of somewhat over-representing the more ecstatic rituals, I'll have to plead guilty where the photos are concerned. Those sessions just happened to provide the most interesting material from the photographer's point of view. My 'sitting' informants have their say in the accompanying texts.

In some orders and in some countries the *Sufis* refer to

themselves as *dervishes*. I will use both words. There is no difference in meaning between a 'sufi' and a 'dervish', except for the fact that a sheikh is a Sufi but not a dervish. The dervishes are his followers.

Secondly, there are no two rival deities, one called Allah and the other God, Gott or Dieu. *Allah* is no more and no less than the Arabic word for God written with a capital G. Christian Arabs use the word 'Allah' just like Muslims do. I will speak of 'God,' except where the text requires 'Allah' as is the case in some passages of Sheikh Zahir's interview.

I thank Sheikh Zahir in Kafr Ibrahim, Egypt; Sheikh Mesud Hadžimejlić and Sheikh Halil Brzina in Sarajevo and their deputies Dr Ćazim Hadžimejlić in Kaćuni and Hišam Hafizović at Vrelo Bune, Bosnia and Herzegovina; Sheikh Arif and his dervish Halil Imami in Struga, Macedonia; Sheikh Mehdi in Rahovec/Orahovac, Kosovo; and Sheikh Salih from Aleppo for their comprehension, trust, and assistance. They supplied me with a wealth of information and kindly tolerated my activity during the rituals. I am also very grateful to their dervishes for their patience. As much as I tried to be unobtrusive, my presence at times must have been a burden to some of them. This makes me appreciate even more the hospitality and kindness with which they treated me.

I couldn't have made the Egyptian sections of this book without the assistance of my old friend, the writer Raouf Musaad Basta. He filled the holes in my gradually deteriorating Arabic, accompanied me to most of the ceremonies, which was a pleasure in itself, and helped me record and interpret the interview with Sheikh Zahir.

The photographer Issa Touma from Aleppo very generously introduced me to the extraordinary rituals that take place in remote corners of northern Syria, on which he has been working himself for the last ten years.

Last but not least, my wife, Mira, cast a critical eye on the one-but-final version of the manuscript and made a number of valuable suggestions to enhance its readability.

I remain indebted to the spirit of Sheikh Erol, who informed me of the peculiarities of Sufism in the Balkans during lengthy sessions at his home in Skopje. He is quoted at length in *God's Lovers*. Sadly, Erol Baba passed away in 2005.

1   Sufism and the Zikr

"The heart rules the brain."
Sheikh Zahir

Mysticism is the expression of a passionate love for God and of the desire to establish an intimate, personal relationship with Him. In Islam this mystic trend, which is found in other religions as well, is called Sufism. Some Sufis say they are in love with God. Their rituals are meant to make the Sufi draw ever closer to God, losing himself in God, and ultimately becoming one with God.

The core of the Sufi ritual is the zikr. This word means 'remembrance' or 'recollection.' It consists essentially of repeating with sincerity and concentration some of God's ninety-nine 'Most Beautiful Names' and related declarations like, 'La ilaha illa Allah,' 'There is no god but God.'

The zikr can take many forms, and there are important differences in this respect among the Sufi orders and among the countries and regions where the orders are active. Certain places and occasions may require special ceremonies and rituals. But the objective is always the same: cleansing the heart of anything but God and filling it with nothing but God.

The ritual can be performed individually or in a group. In the latter the Names will be recited in a rhythmic manner. The participants either sit in a circle swaying their torsos to the rhythm or they stand up, and when they stand up their movement can become a dance, even though they will not use that word for it themselves. The repetition of the Names is often accompanied by singing, and various orders use musical instruments. Though there is always a certain amount of discipline kept by the leader of the zikr, the ritual can become an extremely dynamic and passionate affair, and quite impressive to anyone lucky enough to watch it. The Sufi doesn't dance for God, he dances with God. Whether sitting, standing or dancing, he is removed from this world and finds himself with his Creator, whom he calls his friend or his lover.

Participation in the zikr requires the same ritual purification as the regular obligatory prayers.

As in any meditation, concentration is essential for success. The Bosnian sheikh Halil Brzina defines this as follows: "The effect of the zikr on a person correlates with the intensity of his presence; the intensity of his presence correlates with his love for God; and the intensity of his love for God correlates with the sensitivity of his soul." If the sheikh feels that a participant is thinking of other things, a woman perhaps, he may send him away.

Compared to most Christian denominations Sufism is both very participatory and very physical. Possibly even more than a Christian ordained priest, the sheikh is held to be an intermediary between God and the believer, but he doesn't carry out a ritual by himself watched by a congregation. Rather, he leads the congregation in an effort of their own in which the sheikh himself may participate. Moreover, there is no question of believers sitting or standing while listening to an equally static priest or pastor. In Sufi ritual, the body is an integral part of the person. Its movement is essential to the movement of the spirit toward God. A Sufi sings with his body as well as with his voice.

Though there exists a copious body of theoretical Sufi literature, Muslim mysticism relies on personal experience and practical action like the *zikr* rather than theory. To quote an early master, *"No one will get drunk by reading about wine."* Yet there are those, such as Sheikh Halil, who say that there can be no valid *zikr* without reflection, *fikr*. They believe a Sufi needs some intellectual appreciation of the being he adores before he can meaningfully recollect his name.

With or without intellectual exertion, Sufis are convinced that everything, including rituals and texts, has a hidden, inner meaning. As Sheikh Erol used to say, "The Sunnis – i.e., the non-mystics – occupy themselves with the visible and the tangible; the Sufis devote themselves to the invisible. That is something one can only feel."

The things the Sufis devote themselves to are very

difficult to describe and to define with any degree of exactitude in analytical prose. This explains the omnipresence of poetry in Sufi discourse. Much of this poetry is about love, the obsessive longing of the lover whose infatuation often goes unrequited and then becomes an intolerable burden:

> *I am overcome with love for him;*
> *Cure me!*

sings Hasanayn at the *zikr* for the Prophet's birthday. We shall meet Hasanayn again in Chapter Four.

Another theme is wine and drunkenness, as images of the intoxication induced by the lover's love. With its possibilities of association and analogy, poetry can approximate the ineffable and convey some of the feelings Erol Baba refers to.

Apart from participating in the *zikr*, it is important for a dervish to sit with his sheikh and other pious company in order to imbibe the wisdom and knowledge handed down the chain of sheikhs going back to the Prophet either through the latter's son-in-law Ali or, more rarely, the Prophet's companion Abu Bakr. Together with the *zikr* and other spiritual exercises, this will elevate the soul or ego, the *nafs*, to a higher level, liberating it from all its worldly desires and proclivities. That is the meaning of the famous Sufi maxim, "Die before you die."

Then there is the *adab*, an elaborate set of rules, do's and don'ts, and ways to behave both within one's own community and without. It ranges from fundamental principles of social intercourse to details such as which foot to use to enter the tekke, the building where the dervishes come together (the right foot, of course; the Prophet started every action from the right, including combing his beard. But on leaving the tekke one starts with the left foot).

Lastly, the Sufi effort is carried out in addition to, and not instead of, the duties – like praying and fasting – incumbent on all Muslims by virtue of the Holy Law, the Shari'a. Activities such as the *zikr* are additional, performed on a voluntary basis. The Shari'a remains the basis of the path toward God, the *tarika*, which leads the Sufi toward the realization of the Supreme Reality. The Shari'a is the visible part; the *tarika* and the mystical knowledge acquired through its practices are hidden. The Sufis agree that following the Shari'a is sufficient to be a good Muslim. No-one is under an obligation to seek enlightenment. Some say that the *tarika* can't do without the Shari'a while the Shari'a can do without the *tarika*.

There are hundreds of Sufi orders, for which again the word *tarika* is used, which perpetuate the spiritual habits of their founder saints. The orders are mostly organized on a national basis, and there is very little contact between the national chapters of most orders. Within each country and each order, the Sufis belong to autonomous groups headed by a sheikh or his deputy.

Until the twelfth century CE, Islamic mysticism developed through the efforts of individual sheikhs and their followers, called Sufis on account of their coarse garments made of wool (*suf*). Mostly operating in the margins of society, they conceived, applied, and propagated ideas, approaches, and practices like poverty and asceticism, sobriety and exuberance, divine love and gnosis, and, of course, *zikr* in various forms.

By the end of this formative period, Sufism was ready to be incorporated into mainstream Islam. This happened when saints such as Ahmad al-Rifa'i and their disciples founded the Sufi orders. They offered their members fixed recipes for spiritual activity and discourse based on the discoveries made during the previous half-millennium to guide them in their quest. In this manner the Sufi movement lost some of its experimental creativity, but it was, so to speak, democratized, gaining access to much larger audiences. At some stage a majority of Muslims, including sheikhs at the prestigious al-Azhar institution in Cairo, seem to have belonged to one of the orders. In some countries, such as Senegal, this is still the case.

The non-Sufi Islamic clergy is traditionally loyal to, and even part of, the government of Muslim countries. The Sufi orders have always been parallel structures characterized by a certain degree of independence from the authorities whether lay or clerical. Of course, those authorities will always try to exert as much control over the orders as they can.

Sufism entails a lifelong commitment to the Sheikh and the order. In the words of the famous Turkish poet Yunus Emre:

A person who loves God has a heart which never parts from God;
Unlike lovers of women, he does not love, then leave.

It is not, however, a form of monasticism. Sufism may be a full-time occupation for some sheikhs, but their dervishes marry and have a profession, trade, or occupation. They congregate once or twice a week for a *zikr* session at their lodge or *tekke*, called *tekija* in the Balkans and *zawiya* or *saha* in Egypt. Such a building typically contains one or more rooms for the ritual, a mosque, the tomb of the founder who is considered to be a saint, and, especially in the Balkans, a room for conversation over tea or coffee. But the sessions can be held in any place, and in Egypt they are regularly hosted by the brethren at their homes.

The sheikhs are the pivotal figures in the order. There is a custom for the sheikhhood to be hereditary, but it also happens that someone who is not descended from a sheikh takes over upon a sheikh's death or is allowed to start his own circle. He will be installed in an elaborate ceremony, and is henceforth endowed with the *baraka*, the divine blessing, that distinguished his predecessors. As of that day the new sheikh is practically a free agent, though he will always recognize the spiritual authority of the sheikh who has 'given him the hand,' that is, given him the permission to officiate. The authorities within the orders I have come in contact with seem to possess only nominal powers and to lack both the means and the ambition to control their sheikhs.

The sheikh is entitled to inaugurate and guide the members of the community for which he is responsible, and arbitrates disputes among them. As God's representative, he enjoys great prestige among his followers. Just as he looks after all the spiritual, and often other, needs of his dervishes, the latter owe him absolute obedience and loyalty, 'like a corpse in the hands of the washer of the dead.' The dervish presses his forehead to the palm of the sheikh's hand and kisses it, and occasionally bows at his feet with his forehead touching the ground. In addition to the horizontal solidarity among the brethren, the vertical solidarity between the sheikh and each of the followers is essential for the cohesion of the group.

Usually only men are in evidence in the standing and dancing modes of the *zikr*, but in many orders women can follow the same path as men. They are inaugurated and attend the ceremonies, where they sit at some distance behind the men, silently reciting the Names. Only the Bektashis, the principal Sufi order in Albania but far removed from the other orders with respect to both doctrine and practice, know a free mix of men and women in some of their ceremonies.

The saintly woman Rabi'a al-'Adawiyya, who lived in Basra in the eighth century CE, played an important role in the development of Sufism, being one of the first to teach the doctrine of pure, disinterested love for God, unadulterated by fear of hell or hope for paradise. It is said this conviction prompted her to walk the streets of her hometown with a torch and a bucket of water; the torch to set fire to paradise, the water to quench the flames of hell.

Various kinds of spirituality as well as meditation techniques more or less similar to the *zikr* exist in other religions. So does mysticism. As Tarif Khalidi puts it in *The Muslim Jesus*, "in the Judeo-Christian-Muslim context, the religious identity of a mystical passage selected at random is often untraceable." But an important difference between Islam and most other religions in this regard is that in the former the mystic trend is truly massive. Even though Sufism is by no means an inherently 'popular' or low-class phenomenon, there are countries where it is practiced by the masses rather than by the elites. In Egypt alone, it is claimed, the orders estimate their a combined membership at no less than six million, a minority of the population as a whole but a sizeable one. There are other countries where the Sufis are proportionally as numerous as they are in Egypt. Scratch the surface of any Muslim country with the possible exception of puritanical Saudi Arabia, where the orders were eradicated by the regime, and you will find Sufis. On the whole they don't hide, but they don't manifest themselves frequently, either. When they do, this often happens in less fashionable areas of the city or in remote places in the countryside. A Westerner can live in a Muslim country for years without ever consciously encountering anything connected with Sufism.

The ruling classes often view the orders, especially those with a more ecstatic ritual, with a certain measure of embarrassment; however, the Egyptian government, for one, used to appreciate them as a counterweight to fundamentalist tendencies, and this may still be the case. The fundamentalists regard Sufism, including its veneration of a multitude of saints, as a reprehensible 'innovation,' if not worse.

In theory, a Sufi might be able to follow his path relying only on his master, without the help of saints. In some orders more attention is paid to the saints than in others. But even in the most orthodox orders, the 'Friends of God' – a term that occurs in the Koran, though not with this specific meaning – have a role to play. Whoever joins a Sufi order becomes part of a spiritual network extending from his or her sheikh to the group's founder and numerous other saints, including the originators of the orders, as well as the members of the Prophet's immediate family and ultimately the Prophet himself. Every Sufi community has a list of those to be remembered during the rituals with a prayer for their souls, and whose support is solicited. The *zikr* establishes closeness, not only to God, but to the saints as well. The saints normally manifest themselves in dreams. They are bothered neither by the past nor the future, "knowing neither fear nor grief." The main thing expected from them is intercession with God.

Islam has no central authority responsible for canonizing and uncanonizing saints like the Orthodox and Roman-Catholic branches of Christianity have. Some Friends of God are widely recognized, but most have come into being – and are still coming into being –

locally. They have played a role in the establishment of the Sufi community that remembers them, or they have appeared in dreams with the promise that they will help those who visit them in order to seek their assistance. In the latter case a tomb structure is erected for him or her (there are both male and female saints) and he or she will be venerated as long as they are perceived to perform miracles and, especially, to be successful in pleading with God in favor of the visitors to their tombs. It follows that their cults are subject to ebb and flow and that some disappear altogether to be succeeded by new ones. This is an ongoing process.

There are thousands of holy tombs, and there are tales of miracles connected to each one of them. Many are about the saints' faculty of seeing and knowing facts and events that could not be seen or known in a 'normal' fashion. Others describe visitors being cured of disease or infertility, and there are many testimonies about assistance with the practical problems of daily life such as passing an exam or making a journey.

In the Balkans, where Islam was introduced by the Turks, Sufism carries a distinctly Turco-Persian and, depending on the order, Shi'i flavor. Many orders present here originated in Central Asia, Iran, or Turkey. Arabic is the liturgical language in Koran recitation and in the Most Beautiful Names, but Turkish is used extensively in the *ilahi* hymns sung before, during, and after the *zikr*. *Ilahi* singing is a Turkish custom found in the Balkans but not in the Arabic-speaking regions.

There are also some visible differences between Sufi practice in the Middle East and the Balkans. Unlike their Balkan brethren, Egyptian and Syrian Sufis parade in processions with flags and banners. In Egypt there are numerous annual 'birthday' festivals for the saints, not unlike the medieval saints' fairs in Europe with their combination of religious zeal, trade, and entertainment. In Bosnia there are only a few occasions of that sort, shown in Chapter Six. In Kosovo and Macedonia I don't know of any. In the Balkans many dervishes wear distinctive clothing and headgear during their ceremonies. In Egypt this doesn't seem to be the rule, though there are exceptions such as the Hamidiyya Shadhiliyya, who dress in white for their sessions.

In Bosnia, Sufism does share in a modest Islamic revival but the Sufi presence is less massive than in Egypt. The relationship with the Islamic authorities is proper and often quite cordial. This is facilitated by the orthodoxy of most of the orders, as well as by a shared distaste of the Wahhabi fundamentalists who gained some influence during and after the Bosnian war of 1992–1995. Major Sufi festivities such as those described in Chapter Six are attended by prominent clerics.

***

Until quite recently it was conventional wisdom to think that Sufism did not have much of a future. As Julia Day Howell puts it in *Sufism and the 'Modern' in Islam*, "in the

The Arabic word *huwa*, pronounced *hu* in the Balkans, means "He," i.e., God. Some orders start the *zikr* with "*hu-hu-hu.*" This *hu* is written on the outer wall of the tomb of Sari Saltuk, in the *tekke* on the Buna.

twentieth century some of the most influential scholarly observers of Muslim society ... working in academic environments strongly influenced by post-Enlightenment Protestantism and various forms of modernization theory, all read Sufism as a remnant of traditional village and tribal life. In their view, Sufism was doomed to fade as modernizing social changes increasingly facilitated the displacement of emotive Sufi rituals and mystic practices by the sober scripturalism of city-based legal scholars and exegetes."

Today this analysis seems to have become less tenable than it may have looked before; not unlike longstanding theories about a 'decline in religion.' For one thing, there is nothing specifically rural about Muslim mysticism. Orders like the Nakshbandiyya, the Mawlawiyya, the Khalwatiyya, and the Shadhiliyya have been operating in an urban environment for centuries, and other orders are being introduced into the cities with the influx of people from the countryside.

Apart from that, there exists a great resilience within Sufism due to its inherent flexibility and adaptability. The 'Iron Faith' of Chapter Seven may be on the way out, but the largely autonomous urban sheikhs can and do incor-porate modern notions in their teaching, thus making Sufism relevant to postmodern generations who feel a need for personal and intimate forms of spirituality. One Egyptian friend of mine describes himself as "an atheist Sufi." This is, of course, a contradiction in itself which he is the first to recognize, but it illustrates the attraction of the Sufi approach to those who are put off by legalistic orthodoxy.

***

Whatever their diverse rituals and doctrines, Sufis are extremely tolerant toward one another, toward other forms of Islam and, even though being devout Muslims, toward other religions. The extent of this tolerance will be shown in the interview with an Egyptian sheikh in Chapter Three. Sheikh Osmani, a Sufi healer in Zagreb, says, "God is one, but there are faiths by the hundreds."

In the words of the Greatest Master, Ibn Arabi, "On the Day of Resurrection every human being will see God in the shape in which he worshiped him on earth."

It should not come as a surprise that during all these years, no serious Sufi has ever tried to convert me.

2   Sufi Orders

The Sufis are loosely organized in 'orders,' called *turuk* (singular: *tarika*) in Arabic and tarikat in regions with a Persian or Turkish tradition. The orders are clusters of autonomous groups each headed by a sheikh. In the Balkans there is a belief that the orders as we know them are descended from an original twelve, founded by as many pirs. This might, however, be a construction on the analogy of the twelve Imams of the Shi'a. At present, in any case, there are hundreds of orders, some existing only at the national or regional level, and some spread all around the world.

The members of an order share a spiritual ancestor, the founder saint of the *tarika*. Many orders derive their name from the founder. The awareness of this common ancestry is the main element uniting the members of each Sufi order.

There is a large variety in ritual among the various branches of one order. The *zikr* of the Rifa'is in Egypt is very dissimilar from that of their brethren in Macedonia and Kosovo. The same goes for other orders, like the Halvetis. Sometimes different orders in the same country or region have more in common with one another than with their own counterparts far away.

In the various countries the cohesion within the orders is also uneven. An order may possess a supreme sheikh in the capital but his powers are often of an administrative character, if that. Apart from that, some orders have split into dozens of sub-orders, each with their own sheikh.

Even though on the whole there is little rivalry among the orders, the issue of belonging to a certain *tarika* is important to the Sufis in establishing their identity within Sufism as a whole. Moreover, the orders have preserved some specific features, especially in their character and approach. The Rifa'is have a tendency toward passion and a certain exuberance wherever they are. The Halvetis and Nakshbandis are more disciplined in their rituals, and closer to orthodoxy.

There are four main orders whose rituals are shown or mentioned in this book. They are, alphabetically listed, the following.

The *Kadiriyya* is probably the most widespread Sufi order in the world. There is hardly a Muslim country without a Kadiri presence. It was founded by one of the most prominent Sufi saints ever, Sheikh, or Pir, Abdul

Kadir al-Jilani, also called Gilani or Geylani. He was born in Jilan in Iran and moved to Baghdad when he was eighteen years old. He remained there, first as a student of Islamic law, and, as of his fiftieth year, as principal of a Hanbali madrasa. He became a famous preacher and died in Baghdad in 1166 almost ninety years old. According to the legend that developed after his death, Abdul Kadir would have said: "My foot is on the neck of every saint," and was accepted by all the saints of his time as their leader. His life became a chain of miracles, beginning with Abdul Kadir as a baby refusing his mother's breast at the onset of the Ramadan fast. He converted more than 100,000 thieves and bandits (as well as many Jews and Christians) and turned them into dedicated dervishes.

The ritual differs widely from country to country and from branch to branch, as is normal in the Sufi orders. There is a set of rules of behavior supposed to have been issued by the Pir, some of which are obvious (not to lie, not to be jealous, not to make promises you can't fulfill, not to offend) but one of which stands out in the controversy between Sufism and fundamentalism: "Don't say of anyone that he is an unbeliever or a (religious) hypocrite, because only God knows who is and who isn't."

The Kadiriyya was introduced into the Ottoman Empire by Pir Ismail Rumi, who died in 1631. Shortly afterward the main Kadiri *tekke* in Sarajevo, Hadži-Sinanova *tekija*, was built. It is still active, as are one more Kadiri *tekke* in the same city and one near Jeni Džamija in Travnik.

Outside the *tekkes*, some have permission (*izun*) to lead Kadiri zikrs, and do so at times. The Kadiri zikr is livelier than the Nakshbandi or Khalwati ones, and normally involves a standing (*kiyam*) and sometimes a rotating (*devran*) element; not with individual rotation like the Mevlevis have, but with the circle revolving as a whole.

Numerically the Kadiriyya is the second-largest order in Bosnia, after the Nakshbandiyya.

The *Khalwatiyya* order, whose Macedonian members call themselves Halvetis, was founded by Umar al-Khalwati, who died in Tabriz in 1397. Yahya al-Shirwani, who died in Baku in 1464, is the order's 'Second Pir,' who developed its doctrine and practice and wrote *al-Wird al-sattar*, a litany which is still read in most branches of the order, of which there are hundreds. The Khalwatiyya spread through much of the Ottoman Empire, including the Balkans. Along with the Nakshbandiyya, the Khalwatiyya is one of the least exotic among the Sufi orders. Its foundations are considered to be voluntary hunger, silence, vigil, seclusion (*khalwa*, after which the order is named), zikr, meditation, permanent ritual cleanliness, and tying one's heart to one's sheikh. The Halvetis are very disciplined in their ritual and very close to Islamic orthodoxy.

In Macedonia the Khalwatiyya is the most numerous Sufi order, with active *tekkes* in Ohrid, Struga, and Kičevo. They all belong to the Hayati branch, founded by Pir Mehmet Hayati. Pir Mehmet was initiated as a Khalwati sheikh in Serres by Sheikh Huseyn Rumi in 1776 and subsequently settled in Ohrid.

The *Nakshbandiyya*, named after Baha al-Din Nakshband,

who died in 1389, originated in Bukhara in Transoxania. It remained preponderant in Central Asia, and spread both to India and the Turkish-speaking regions, including the Ottoman Empire where its Khalidi branch became the paramount order in the nineteenth century. It never made much of an inroad in the Arabic-speaking lands.

The Nakshbandiyya's insistence on sober respect for the Shari'a made it acceptable to religious scholars, bureaucrats, and men of letters. Their *zikr* was *khafi*, that is, conducted in silence. In Bosnia, where its adherents call themselves Nakshibendi, the order's first *tekke* was established in Sarajevo in 1472, and over time the order developed into the largest in the country. Around 1800 the silent *zikr* was abolished in a change brought about by Husejin Baba Zukić, 'the Bosnian Second Pir,' who came from the Fojnica area, was educated in Istanbul, and then studied with Nakshbandi sheikhs in Konya, Bukhara, and Samarkand. He worked and died at Vukeljići in Central Bosnia. His disciple Sheikh Sirri Sikirić appointed Hadži Mejli Baba as the head of the *tekke* at Vukeljići, where he died in 1854. Mejli Baba's descendants, the Hadžimejlići, are still prominent among the Sufi sheikhs of Bosnia.

The *Rifa'iyya*, called Rufaija in the Balkans, are one of the largest and most active Sufi orders in the world, especially at the popular level. They are active in Egypt, where they are the most numerous order, Iraq, Syria, Turkey, around the Indian Ocean, and in the Balkans, especially in Kosovo. The order was established by a contemporary of Abdul Kadir al-Jilani, Sidi (or Pir) Ahmad al-Rifa'i. He lived in the marshlands of Southern Iraq between 1106 and 1182, leaving his village of Umm 'Abida, or Umm 'Ubayda, only for a pilgrimage to Mecca and Medina. Sidi Ahmad was a descendant of the Prophet Muhammad through both his parents, whose family trees could be traced back to Muhammad's grandsons Husayn and Hasan, respectively; hence his nickname of "Abul 'Alamayn", the Man with the Two Flags. He was neither a writer – though the order's special litany, *al-Hizb al-Rifa'i*, is attributed to him – nor an original thinker. His fame rests on his extraordinary personality. Right from the start, and probably following the founder's own example, his order was known for its passion and flamboyance. Its members performed feats like riding lions, walking on burning coals, and piercing their bodies with iron. In Egypt and some other countries the Rifa'i dervishes are credited with power over scorpions and snakes.

Though the order was introduced into the Balkans at an early date, the present-day branch in Kosovo was established only in 1860 by Hadži Sheikh Musa, who was initiated in Istanbul. He established a *tekke* at Gjakova/Djakovica, and the *tarikat* spread from there to Rahovec/Orahovac, Prizren, Mitrovica, and a number of towns in Albania. Most of its members are ethnic Albanians. A predominantly Turkish branch had been established in Skopje, Macedonia, by Mehmed Baba Haznadar in 1818. Most Turks left the former Yugoslavia during the last century, and today the Macedonian Rifa'is largely belong to the Roma ethnicity.

3 A Sufi on Sufism: Interview with Sheikh Zahir

Sheikh Zahir Abdallah Ahmad Abu Zaghlal al-Rifa'i is in his mid-fifties. He has been the spiritual leader of a few thousand Sufis since his father died about twenty-five years ago. In Egypt there are thousands of local sheikhs just like him.

This conversation took place on Saturday, February 24th, 2007 in Bilbeis. It was the day after we had been at an extraordinarily passionate zikr in the village of Suwa and, almost to the day, twenty years after our first meeting.

I first asked the sheikh to speak about Sufism in general terms.
SZ: The Prophet has decreed that all should live in security and peace. There should be no hate or prejudice or envy against anyone. The Jews are Jews and the Christians are Christians. Each one of them has established his own way of worshiping our Lord. Everyone has his own line connecting him with God. Which is why the Prophet ordered that during wars, when his men entered a town, places of worship should be protected just as there should be no killing of old people and women or burning of houses or killing of children.

With the Islamists this is different. They have a different discourse. But violence, hatred, and fanaticism are not a part of Islam. Why do they attack the Sufis? They call us "the soft cheek of Islam." But the Prophet himself was like that! As God said to Muhammad, "If you had been rude and hard-hearted, people would have deserted you." Islam is peace, love, and brotherhood. This was the way of our saints. The basis of their behavior toward everyone was that they were God's creatures. One has to respect God's creatures. If I don't respect God's creatures I don't respect God. You need love and brotherhood and justice and sympathy toward God's creatures.

For instance, a man, ninety-nine years old, came to the prophet Abraham. Abraham invited him for a meal. Then he asked him, "What is your religion?" When Abraham learned that the man did not worship God he canceled the invitation and dismissed him. Then God sent Gabriel down and said, "Tell Abraham this: This man is a pagan who doesn't believe in me, but I have had patience with him for ninety-nine years. Can't you suffer him for one hour?" One has to respect God's creatures. God will draw up the final account, not you. You just have to do as you are told.

Muslims remember God (perform the zikr) to come

closer to God. *Nawafil* are pious actions and activities that are not obligatory. For example, fasting during Ramadan is an obligation, but voluntary fasting after Ramadan is *nawafil*. The five daily prayers are an obligation, but if a person then continues praying, that is *nawafil*. If he performs *nawafil* he will be drawn closer to God. The *zikr* is one of the *nawafil*. God has said, "My servant comes closer to me by *nawafil*; the (best) way to come closer to God is the *zikr*."

The *zikr* is dear to God. When a person remembers God – "*La ilaha illa Allah*," "Allah," or any of the Names by which he remembers God – he remembers him with his tongue. And then the remembrance reaches the heart.

The heart is like a vessel. It is filled with the remembrance of God. It is filled with the light of God. When the heart is full of God's light, it will be in a state of intense love. Love with God. Totally. The meaning of the word "Allah" belongs to the realm of divine light.

Our saints and sheikhs seize the dervish, and plant "Allah" in his heart. They do this because the heart is the engine of every human being. In the words of the Prophet, "In the body there exists a certain part. If it is healthy then the whole body is. If it is sick, so is the whole body. That is the heart."

In this heart enters God's light. The seat of man's intentions is the heart. All of man's intentions reside in the heart. The heart is the starting point for good and for evil. The heart rules the brain. The heart is the engine of everything. When a person remembers God, God's light fills the heart. Therefore the hearts of those who know,

those who have reached God, have eyes. These eyes see what others don't see. This is the clairvoyance (*basira*) of the believer. Beware of the clairvoyance of the believer! He has eyes that see by God's light.

Can anyone reach this state, or is it only in the grasp of the sheikh and the dervishes?
SZ: Whoever is sincere with God will see. God removes from his heart the darkness, the curtains that hide the heart from God. Love of possessions, love of women, love of the world ... all these are barriers. When a person connects with God he leaves all that behind and he does without it, on God's path.

Does this only happen during the zikr?
SZ: The *zikr* is only a means, a means to reach God. "Allah, Allah, Allah" fills the heart with God's light. And when it is filled with God's light, the light overflows and the whole body is illuminated with God's light, but in a human form.

This is proven by what happened yesterday [as Sheikh Zahir was dozing off before the start of the *zikr*, and was woken up by a boy who touched him in passing] when the child touched me, I said, "Allah." A normal person wouldn't have said this. Why? By the grace of God my heart is full of light. The heart is like a vessel. If a pot is only half full of honey and you touch it, you will touch glass. But if we fill it to the brim, will you then touch glass or honey? You will touch honey, because it is overflowing. When you touch someone who is engaged in the zikr, he will say, "Allah." After the heart is filled up and the ego (nafs) is purified, basira happens. Beware of this clairvoyance of the believer! He sees by God's light, because his heart has become God's house. God says, "Neither heaven nor earth is my abode, but the heart of my believing servant is."

God can't be defined by any size, but He is light. God is light. When you have this light inside you, you see through the darkness and you see the hidden world. Such a person sees what is behind the surface. This is a seeing but not with the eyes. Basira is given to those who are close to God and who make an effort.

Whoever takes part in the zikr experiences the hadra, or zikr session, with God. It is called a hadra, literally meaning 'presence' because of the presence of the heart, the presence of God in the heart. The hadra is a person's presence with God. With God he leaves everything else and forgets about everything else. The spirit ascends to the presence of God. It connects with God, through God. It is a connection like a mobile telephone. I dial the number. There is no wire, but the number comes through. That is to say, it is the right number. And then you talk. There is no wire, but there is a radiation. There is a connection that can't be seen, but it can be felt. So that person is present with God, and we don't see it. But God is there. God is in contact with him and steers him. Because he has made contact and dialed the right number, and the number has answered. If the battery is not full, if the card is empty, it won't work, but if the battery is all right and the connection is good, then he will come in contact with God. So there is purity and there is love and there is sincerity, and there is pleasure with God.

Sidi Ahmad al-Rifa'i, the founder of the Rifa'iyya order, had inside him a fire of love that was stronger than worldly fire. During his hadras he started a blazing fire, and he made his dervishes enter the fire. "Go into the fire and remember God!" They extinguished the fire with their own fire. Likewise, when they threw the prophet Abraham into the fire, he said, "Be cool and peaceful to Abraham!" and it didn't burn him. People asked God, "If people disobey you, how will you punish them?" And He said: "I will punish them with the fire of the lovers who love my beauty." The fire of God's lovers is stronger than the fire of the world.

'Umar ibn al-Farid, Rabi'a al-'Adawiyya, all of them lived with God and loved God and forgot about everything else. Rabi'a said, "May whatever links me with You be whole, and let whatever links me with the world be shattered. Your love is all that counts. Whatever is on earth is only dust."

The saints lived with God so that God was pleased and they came near to God and they pleased God and he was happy with them. Gods words prove this: "My servant, obey me and then I shall make you a lordly servant who says to something: 'Be!' and it will be." That person has reached that stage by virtue of engaging in the zikr. And when he sits in a state of nearness to God there is joy and the heart delights in God, and there is no delight like it. They lived with God. When a person experiences love in the zikr he is not here anymore. He is in contact with God. Light has been kindled inside him, and if he persists at that level and holds on to it, he will stay there. Whether the saints moved or rested, it came from God.

There is a miracle by Ahmad al-Rifa'i. There was a religious scholar from Basra who was opposed to al-Rifa'i and his spiritual states. He watched the movement in the zikr, as we were doing last night in Suwa. There was a participant in the zikr who made a violent movement, and the scholar asked: "Is this not forbidden or reprehensible?" Rifa'i said: "Yes. Whoever remembers God can't be violent like that." So the sheikh summoned the dervish and asked him, "Why were you behaving in that way?" The latter answered, "There is a guest among us from Basra, who left his wife and daughter at home. A thief came and robbed the house and wanted to rape the women, so I killed him." The sheikh asked, "Who around here is from Basra?" The guest replied, "I." So they went to Basra, to the house of the scholar, and they found the thief killed, and the wife and daughter who said: "Thank that man, he protected us from the thief." The scholar believed in the miracle, he returned to Sidi Ahmad al-Rifa'i, and became one of his followers.

How about "disappearing in God (al-fana' fi-l-llah)?"
SZ: In such a case a person has lost his own identity in God's. God then takes complete care of him. The person

has surrendered himself. He doesn't have any strength of his own anymore. He is like a political refugee.

Is that exceptional?
SZ: No. It can happen to anyone. It is a matter of effort. Whoever makes the effort will succeed.

Is it a gift from God?
SZ: There is an element of that. Everything comes from God. There is no success except through God. There are Jews, Muslims, Christians, Zoroastrians ... that is God's work. He has lined up his servants as he wishes. He chose this for this one and that for the other. That is not our business. Everyone makes his own connection. He follows his own direction. It is not our business. What we do isn't anyone else's business, either. It is no use looking at the others while we drive, lest we cause an accident.

What is the role of women in the order?
SZ: As you saw, there are female dervishes, who are much respected. They sit, they are respected, but as is the case during the daily prayers, there is no mixing of men and women. They are on one side, we are on the other.

Do they take part in the zikr?
SZ: No. They sit and they remember God on their own, with full concentration, to the rhythm of the zikr. But mixing within the zikr itself? No.

Can they reach the same spiritual stage?

SZ: Certainly. Rabi'a al-'Adawiyya reached it. A woman can reach it by prayer, by recitation.

There are various forms of zikr: sitting, standing, and so on. . .

SZ: There are different kinds of sport. There is football, there is handball. . . As long as you don't mix them up. That would be wrong.

Who is present during the hadra?

SZ: God is always present, here, in the heart. But the saints may attend; secretly, through their light. Who sees them? The spirit feels it. First, contact is established between the spirits. After that it depends on the degree of enlightenment. If the participant in the *zikr* is at a high level of enlightenment, he can see them. Then he sees the saints. Suppose President Hosni Mubarak visits Bilbeis. Can I go and see him? Of course not. The people in charge can go and see him, not the common people. There are people who can see him and people who can't. Who will get permission? Special people in special positions.

Do the saints mediate between us and God?

SZ: Yes. The Koran says, "Ask an expert." For example, if God wishes that I visit Holland [we had been speaking about that possibility], I have to go to the embassy. I have to get a visa. All step by step. There is a door, an entry, and it is no use trying to avoid that.

Is the saint or the sheikh the doorkeeper?

SZ: Yes. The sheikh is a saint (*wali*), as well.

Is it possible to participate in the zikr without taking part in the litany (wird) that is recited ahead of it?

SZ: The *wird* is a preparation for the participant. If someone starts playing a match without practicing beforehand, he may get a muscle cramp. The *wird* takes care of the preparation of the spirit. It enters inside. So, it will prepare the presence with God for fifty percent, or seventy percent, or a hundred. You can say the *wird* in any language. The only important thing is its meaning. Are there languages that God doesn't understand? He created everything!

Can a person perform the zikr only with a group, or by himself as well?

SZ: The zikr is only a means, not an end in itself. It is a means to reach God. In the days of the Prophet people were in the vicinity of the Prophet, and the electric charge of the faith was very high. Everyone was a *hadra* in himself! Then the Prophet died. After that, people were distracted by the affairs of the world. Then they started to perform the zikr in a group: "Allah, Allah, Allah." They also needed something to put them in the right mood. There was a singer, who was making his music. He began to sing poetry that drew the spirits closer to God. He became a *munshid* (a singer in the *zikr*) for them, who relaxed their spirits and made them move, like a dancing girl who begins to move. What makes her move? Hearing the music makes her move. Now that is hearing with the ears. When the spirits listen to the *zikr* it makes them move in a similar fashion.

Was yesterday's zikr a special one for you?
SZ: Yes. When the *munshid* is in contact with God he moves the spirits more. And the force with which he remembers those songs moves them still more. It is as if an engine has fifty or sixty or a hundred horse power. The stronger the engine, the stronger its pull.

At the start of the *zikr* the participants will say, "Allah." After a while this becomes "ah-ah." Why? Because all perfection is defective, and every defect can be perfect. The word "Allah" is perfect as to its pronunciation. But it is defective in meaning. "Allaaah" is generated by the tongue for ninety percent, and for ten percent by the heart. Now, we want it all to come from the heart. The heart is the axis. So what do we say? We say "Allah" with the heart: "ah-ah-ah." The tongue is immobilized, and it comes from the heart. The light comes straight from the heart. There is no cover, no cellophane, nothing. So "ah-ah-ah" becomes perfect in meaning though it is deficient in terms of words.

When in such a state, do you still hear the munshid's *words?*
SZ: Yes. This is because the *munshid's* words move our deepest feelings. What kind of happiness do you feel then? It is like a soldier in the war. When he hears the words of the national songs they lift his morals. But when there are no national songs . . .

In the days of the Old Sheikh [Sheikh Zahir's grandfather, the founder of this community], a *zikr* was going on like the one you saw yesterday, only with ten times as many people. Then the sheikh said about one of the participants, "Remove him from the *zikr*! He is not with God. In his heart he is thinking of a woman. Take him out." You see what insight he had! You see how he saw through people's hearts? They removed the fellow because the *zikr* is remembrance of God, and it can't be associated with other things.

Can the head of the Rifaʻi order in Egypt issue instructions to you?
SZ: We have to follow the Sheikh's instructions.

What do those instructions concern?
SZ: He can instruct us, say, to follow the Shariʻa.

Does he check?
SZ: To be frank, he should [examine our actions]. He should control us. But there is no supervision and there is no [examination]. So, everyone can do his own thing as long as he stays within the general lines. But there are many who stray beyond the general lines. Like a student without a teacher. He has his books, but will he study? Will he pass? There is a need for a teacher to be in control.

You don't seem to be in need of a teacher. Didn't you tell me once that your [deceased] father and grandfather act as your guides?
SZ: Yes. They supervise us and they even check the details.

By God's grace, my father and grandfather come in dreams. They come all the time.

I will tell you of a miracle about control and detailed checking. On one of my trips I went to a village called Kilometer Seventeen on the road to Isma'ilia. My grandfather visited me in a dream, saying: "You are on your way to Seventeen. Well, tell Abdulhamid Abu Arafa over there that he has to put the words "our lord" before "Muhammad" in the call to prayer: "I witness that our lord Muhammad is God's messenger." [This wording is proper to the sheikh and his followers; normally "our lord" is not part of the call to prayer.] I was certain that this was a valid dream. Now this Abdulhamid was a bit of a tense man who might get angry if I told him this, but I thought, I will tell him, it can't be helped. I stayed for three days, and when I was about to leave I thought, let me tell him now, so if he gets angry I will be on my way. So I said, "I had a dream. The Old Sheikh visited me, saying, "Tell Abdulhamid that he should use the words "our Lord."" He said, "But that is what I do all the time." I said, "I know." But then Abdulhamid said, "Wait. Three days ago, the day you saw him in your dream, I said in the call to prayer, "I witness that our Lord Muhammad is God's messenger," but then during the prayer I said, "I witness that Muhammad is God's messenger." Those who were sitting with me in the prayer didn't even notice. All right. The sheikh is dead. How could he know? He came, dead and all? What are you trying to tell me?"

You see the supervision and the attention to detail?

One day, after the death of my father and grandfather, when I had assumed the leadership of the community (khilafa), my grandfather visited me in a dream. He mentioned some events that happened on the day I took over from my father, and said: "Do you remember what happened on that day? That was the night when I obtained the official confirmation of your khilafa from the Prophet." So they keep track of us in every respect.

The sheikh loved everything. People, animals, birds; he loved them all because God created them. The Old Sheikh used to feed the dogs around the place where we meet. One day, long after the sheikh died – and now you will see another example of control – there were heavy rains. The roads had not yet been paved so there was mud everywhere. The sheikh appeared to the cleaning lady, he woke her up at two in the morning, and said, "Get up and feed the dogs behind the house of Sheikh Abdulhamid." She woke me up, and I asked her, "Where are the dogs now?" She said, "Let us light a lantern," so we went along slowly and we found a lot of dogs. They were very hungry. We fed them and went home.

Do you have a message for our western readers?
SZ: As Muslims we love all religions. Our objective is love and peace. As Sufis we love all people, each one on his own path. God created them like this. We love all people. We strive for love and respect, because our message is in the Koran: "The Messenger [Prophet Muhammad] believes in what has been revealed to him by his Lord, and

all the faithful believe in God, his angels, his scriptures and his messengers. We do not make any distinction among the messengers, any one of them."

So we respect all religions. If we did not respect all messengers and Prophets, our Islam would not be complete.

Sheikh Zahir blessing a baby.

Sheikh Zahir's saha at Kafr Ibrahim.

4   Dancing with God (Egypt)

It takes about two hours to get from Cairo to Bilbeis in one of the Peugeot service taxis branded 'flying coffins' on account of the accidents caused by their drivers. Another taxi will take you to the village of Kafr Ibrahim, where the Rifa'i Sheikh Zahir Abu Zaghlal has a compound which he calls his *saha*. This is where he lives, where his father and grandfather are buried, and where he congregates with his dervishes. These are a few thousand in number, of all ages. Most of them are peasant farmers living in a number of villages in the area, but some are found elsewhere, as well – in Cairo, in Ismailia, and even far away in Upper Egypt. The sheikh visits them on a regular basis.

I had an unusually lucky day when I met Sheikh Zahir, in March, 1987, only weeks after embarking upon the preparations for a book on the Egyptian saints' festivals, the *moulids*. The book appeared three years later. At this point in time the sheikh, accompanied by a few dozen of his followers, was visiting the *moulid* of the Sayyida Zaynab, a member of the Prophet's family. This they did every year, and then they stayed for a week in the ancient Sarghitmish mosque, one of the most beautiful in Cairo,

in the neighborhood of the tomb of the Sayyida. I believe this is still their custom.

That afternoon I walked into the mosque, where the sheikh and his people were resting from the previous night's *zikr* and preparing for the following one. They gave me tea and I took some photos. Sheikh Zahir was thirty-five years old. He was very friendly and welcoming right from the start, and soon became a good friend with whom I stayed in contact over the years. He proved to be a valuable informant, willing and able to explain the Sufi approach to life and religion in easily comprehensible terms. Like other Sufi sheikhs I have met, he is at the same time a dedicated spiritual leader and a practical person with a good sense of humor. Twenty years later he gave me the interview reproduced in the previous chapter.

I saw him and his dervishes regularly during 1987 and 1988, both at the *saha* and at various *moulids*. In 1992 I brought him the book on the *moulids*. He went through the photos and remarked that I should have paid more attention to the *haraka*, the collective movement so typical of Sufi ceremonies in Egypt. When I was there again in 1994, I traveled up and down the Delta for most of the night until I found him at a minuscule *moulid* in a village with no electricity. While working on the present book, which is in large part about the *haraka*, I watched a number of his *zikrs*, again: in 2004 during the month of Ramadan, when they perform at least one every night; in February 2007, when we recorded the interview; and in March, 2008, around the Prophet's birthday, when there is another period of enhanced ritual activity.

The Ramadan sessions were hosted at various villages by those brethren who could afford it. They started with the *iftar* dinner that breaks the fasting at sunset, the guests sitting on the floor around large metal platters on which rice, soup, vegetables and meat were served. This was followed by a lengthy prayer, and then came the *zikr* ceremony, the *hadra*. It had the same components as during the year – a forceful common sitting recitation of *al-hizb al-rifa'i*, the order's litany, several hours of *zikr*, and at the end concluding prayers, tea, and sometimes a piece of fruit. The end of Ramadan was celebrated with a massive *zikr* in the *saha* followed by a meal.

The period leading up to the birthday of the Prophet saw numerous *hadras* as well, hosted by varying members of the group. They started around eight or nine at night and were followed by the customary supper. The festivity at the *saha* on the night preceding the *moulid* was again a massive one. It started around nine with a litany, followed by a meal, followed by another litany, and finally a fervent *zikr*, which went on until midnight. There was tea and some sweets, and then all the participants disappeared into the night. The next morning many of them would be toiling in their fields.

The *zikr* goes through cycles of about half an hour each, during which the rhythm gradually accelerates. The movement essentially consists of an inclination to the right with the upper part of the body, a straightening, an inclination to the left, another straightening, and back to the right. As the movement accelerates, it is simplified to turning right and left. The feet remain in the same place. As long as the rhythm is slow, "*la ilaha illa Allah*," with its four emphases, is the main Name, and every *zikr* starts with it. As the tempo increases, the Names get shorter: "*Allah hayy; hayy, hayy*," and the like, articulated or not. At the end of a cycle there is no pause, but the music takes off again right away in the slow rhythm of the beginning.

In Egypt the dynamics of the *zikr* depend very much on the abilities of the singer, the *munshid*. The sheikh, who actively participates in the movement, largely delegates the conduct of the *zikr* to the *munshid*, even though the latter is bound by subtle instructions from the sheikh as the *zikr* progresses. Unlike the custom in Bosnia, where the sheikh does not participate himself and where the singers only accompany the recitation of the Names using existing songs, these *munshids* are expected to improvise. They will use excerpts of classical Sufi poetry, but they are not kept to any specific text. They use the local dialect in their songs, which will contain whatever their mind comes up with in the context of the ritual. A good singer makes the *zikr*. Sheikh Zahir has two excellent munshids; the younger one, Naggar, is practically always there, and the older one, an Upper Egyptian named Hasanayn, born around 1922, often joins in and then keeps going for hours. They can be supported by other dervishes with good voices, and occasionally by the sheikh himself. Sheikh Zahir's grandfather did away with the use of musical instruments.

The music meanders round the continuous repetition of the Names with songs about the Prophet, the saints, mystical love, wine and intoxication.

> *"I have grabbed the cup with my hand,*
> *With my hand,*
> *(Prophet), fill it up!"*

sings Hasanayn at the birthday of the Prophet;

> *"Ahmad, oh! Ahmad,*
> *Light of God,*
> *Only you have drunk the cup from the highest of the high.*
> *From the highest of the high drank the Prophet."*

Ahmad, like Mustafa, is one of the names sometimes used to refer to the Prophet Muhammad.

***

Sheikh Zahir, born in 1952, radiated a gentle but unquestioned authority, and his presence was very important to his dervishes. Upon his arrival all would get up and welcome him with a song. Apart from officiating at the zikrs the sheikh spent considerable time in other duties, counseling people from the village, blessing babies, settling disputes. All the time, he was exceedingly kind and attentive to those in the room where he happened to sit. When food was passed around he would offer them morsels of it with a personal word. His mobile phone kept ringing with the calls of followers in need of his advice.

Since there were many who wished to host a session during Ramadan, there were evenings when two or three hadras were held in different villages. The sheikh then drove from one to the other and every time plunged into the zikr without any reserve, leading his dervishes to even higher degrees of rapture. His stamina was extraordinary.

During the rest of the year the movement was just as intensive as it had been during the holy month of Ramadan. One of the most passionate zikrs I witnessed took place at the Bedouin village of Suwa in February 2007. The sheikh reached such a state where he threw off his turban and his outer clothes, keeping only his undergarment. The next day he told me that this had been due to the singing of the munshid Hasanayn. The same thing happened at the Prophet's moulid, inspired by the same singer. The sheikh's example was not followed by others.

Sheikh Zahir's grandfather and father are buried within the saha. Whenever the zikr is held there, normally after the noon prayer on Friday, the tombs are visited by the sheikh and the brethren ahead of the ceremony. There are numerous miracle stories about Abu Zaghlal, the *saha's* founder, some of which show his love and respect for animals [like the founder of the Rifa'i order, Sidi Ahmad, who saw a cat sleeping on a corner of his mantle when he needed it to go praying. He took a knife and carefully cut off the corner to make sure the cat would not be disturbed].

Abu Zaghlal abolished the piercing of the body with iron pins during the *zikr*, a custom that was frequent among Egyptian Rifa'is in earlier times and is still prevalent today in Kosovo and northern Syria. He deemed it to be superfluous ostentation.

Al-hizb al-rifa'i, the litany recited as a warming-up to the *zikr*, is held to have healing and protective properties. If read by a sheikh or a senior dervish over a container of water in which the reader dips a finger, drinks a little, and spits it back, the water will protect against snakes and scorpions, heal sickness, and dispense *baraka*, the blessing associated with holy people and places. The litany is recited at full voice by all participants, and takes about a quarter of an hour to read.

Sheikh Zahir has two sons, named after his father and his grandfather, respectively. Abdallah, who attends most of the *hadras*, is his prospective successor. Ahmad is a computer technician in Bilbeis.

Abu Zaytoun. The *zikr* is taking place in the background. Sheikh Zahir is counseling a man from the village. Women and girls are watching.

Female dervishes praying at the *saha*.

After prayers at the *saha*, Sheikh Zahir and his dervishes leave the
mosque singing, on their way to pay their respect at the tombs of

Chanting the *hizb al-rifaʻi* at Basatin. The Sheikh keeps a finger in a
jar of water, which will thus acquire healing power.

Chanting the *hizb* at the *saha*.

Zikr at the home of Abdul Ghassan Abdallah (front, right) at 'Izbet
al-Sa'iba.

Zikr at Basatin.

Zikr at Kafr Abu Nagm.

Zikr at the end of Ramadan in the *saha*.

Zikr at the *saha* for the Prophet's Birthday. Sheikh Zahir has thrown off his turban and will soon shed his upper garment as well.

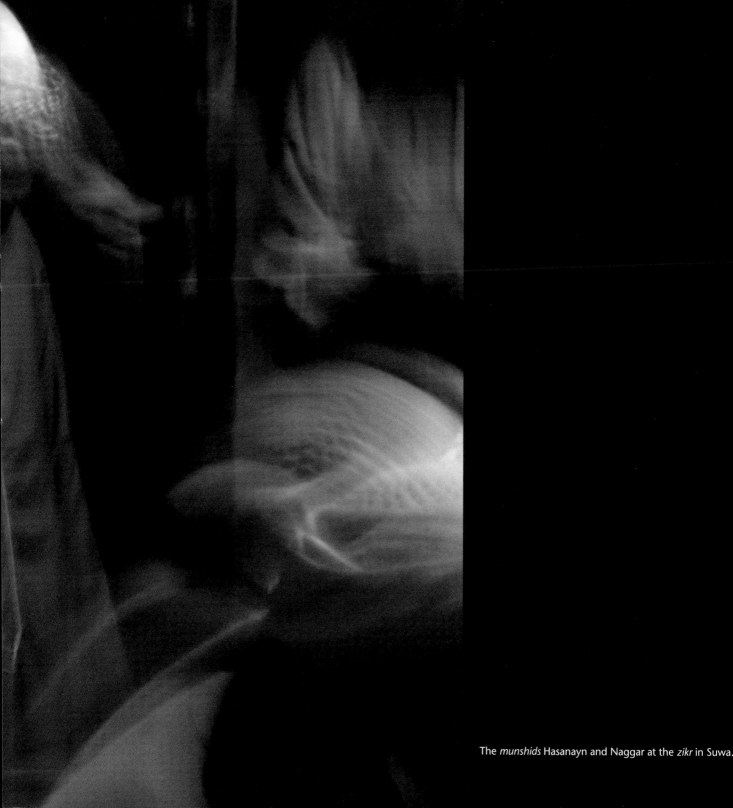

The *munshids* Hasanayn and Naggar at the *zikr* in Suwa.

Sheikh Zahir at the *zikr* in Suwa.

Zikr in Suwa.

Women and children partaking of the dinner. At the back is the
entrance to the room containing the tombs of the sheikh's father
and grandfather.

Pieces of dessert carrying the *baraka* of the sheikh, who has cu
are handed around after the *zikr* for the Birthday of the Proph
Since 2007, the walls of the *saha* have been painted green.

Kissing the sheikh's hand at the end of the *hadra*. The woman is on her way home, carrying her shoes. The man to the right of the sheikh is keeping the clothes that the latter threw off during the *zikr*.

The *tekke* at the source of the Buna river.

5 Sitting with God (Bosnia-Herzegovina, Macedonia, Kosovo)

One of the loveliest spots in the Balkans is situated in Herzegovina near the village of Blagaj, not far from the city of Mostar. There is a sheer rock face which may be a hundred meters high. Swallows, pigeons, and other birds fly in and out of its many crevices. At the foot of the rock the river Buna comes into the world at full force, its clear blue waters filtered by the sediments within the mountain. It joins up with the Neretva river some eight kilometers downstream.

Right next to the source of the Buna, *Vrelo Bune*, there is an elegant little Sufi meeting place, a *tekke* which in its present shape dates from around 1850. It contains two tombs, one of which – along with another seven tombs in as many places in the Balkans and Anatolia – is ascribed to Sari Saltuk, a legendary warrior-saint reputed to have brought Sufism to the Balkans even before the arrival of the Turks in the fourteenth century.

Over the course of time the *tekke* has been home to various Sufi orders: Bektashi, Khalwati, Kadiri. The building survived the Bosnian war thanks to the protection against artillery fire provided by the surrounding rock. In 2006, after the building had been out of regular religious use for years, a Nakshbandi group began congregating there on Thursday and Sunday evenings for a *zikr* led by the youngest Sufi deputy sheikh (*vekil*) in Bosnia and Herzegovina, Hišam efendi Hafizović, born in 1979. Hišam studied Islamic theology in Sarajevo. He is an intelligent, serious, and friendly person, well respected by his dervishes, be they older or younger. His excellent relationship with the Islamic community is illustrated by his appointment as *imam* of the mosque in nearby Blagaj, which involves leading the ritual prayers and pronouncing the Friday sermon, with the aim of making it possible for him to conduct the *zikr* at the *tekke*, as well.

When I asked Hišam for permission to take photos of his group, he referred me to Sheikh Halil Brzina, who is responsible for the activities at the Buna *tekke* along with another ten circles in different places run by *vekils* such as Hišam efendi. Sheikh Halil graciously received me at his own Mejtaš *tekke* in Sarajevo near the mosque of Sarač Ismail. He gave his blessing to the project on condition that I didn't intend to photograph the sessions he conducted himself in Sarajevo, since he felt that this might interfere with his followers' concentration. I would be very welcome to watch the sheikh's *zikr* without a camera.

Sheikh Halil, born near Stolac in Herzegovina in 1953, is an impressive man of action and a very eloquent preacher, as I witnessed at the occasion of a sitting *zikr* he conducted during the Ajvatovica pilgrimage (see Chapter Six). He is proud of his family, which has a warrior tradition rather than a Sufi one, and of his own action in the Bosnian army during the 1992–1995 war. First introduced to Sufism in the 1970s by fellow students from Jordan and Palestine during his management training in Novi Sad and Beograd, he joined the Nakshbandi order in the 1980s while still employed by the steelworks in Zenica. He was inaugurated as a sheikh by Sheikh Mesud Hadžimejlić in 1993. He has never ceased to be a manager. He built and renovated a number of mosques and *tekkes*, among which is the 'war mosque' on Mount Igman near Sarajevo, where on the first Friday in August a prayer session is held for the martyrs of the Bosnian war.

Sheikh Halil is by no means the only Nakshbandi leader who has taken up arms in the defense of his country or people. The epic resistance against the Russian conquest of the North Caucasus in the nineteenth century was very much a Nakshbandi effort. Nakshbandi sheikhs also fought in the Russo-Turkish War of 1870, during the First World War, and during the Turkish War of Independence.

Sheikh Halil seems to be somewhat stricter than others with regard to the *zikr* ritual, which in Nakshbandi custom involves a sitting mode only, and not a standing or dancing one. He will occasionally participate in a standing *zikr* as described in the next chapter, but will not lead one. He has, however, not interfered with the standing *zikr* that has traditionally taken place during the May pilgrimage at the *tekke* on the Buna. His dervishes are allowed to take part in standing *zikrs* on other occasions as well, where they can be recognized by the red fezzes which the sheikh has established as distinctive 'Bosnian' headgear for his followers instead of the habitual white or green caps.

In an interview for *Kelamu'l Šifa*, 3, Sheikh Halil stresses the importance of faithful adherence to the Shari'a in a visible manner in order to acquire inwardly the light of true religion; believing with the intellect is converted into believing with the heart. Sheikh Halil likes to keep his feet close to the ground, and doesn't share the disdain for the affairs of this world traditionally professed by so many Sufis. "Don't flee from the world to fly around in the heavens! The world has been given, heaven has been promised; don't lose the given, because you'll lose both given and promised!" Apart from that, "Knowledge is the greatest miracle... The dream of a learned person is worth more than the devotions of an ignorant one." Zikr and *fikr*, reflection, are like the two wings without which the bird can't fly, Sheikh Halil says.

Sheikh Halil takes an active interest in his people as they move through the stages of *muhib* (aspirant), *murid* (dervish), and eventually *vekil*. Once a year, in the month of June, he comes over to inaugurate new dervishes in a ceremony in which they swear allegiance to the sheikh and the Nakshbandi order. On that occasion he determines the *vird*, the 'homework' each of them has to do in the form of certain Names to be recited on a daily basis, apart from the biweekly *zikr* at the *tekke*. Over time, the *vird* can be adjusted according to the dervish's progress. The sheikh visits the *tekke* at other times during the year, as well.

The *tekke* on the Buna is no more than a two-hour drive away from my village in Dalmatia, so I could come over quite regularly during the summer of 2007. Normally the sessions take place in quasi-darkness, but when it became clear that under these conditions I would have to use a flash, the dervishes were kind enough to keep the light on and even to turn it up. What mattered to them most was that Sheikh Halil had agreed to the project. Only one of them asked me not to take photos of him, because he feared that this might distract his attention from the ritual. Since due to the small size of the room this would have been difficult to do all of the time, he was satisfied with my promise to make an effort not to include him.

The sessions in the *tekke* take place in two carpeted rooms on the second floor, one for the men and one for the women. The women follow the *zikr* through a microphone. Until recently they shared one room, but it was rather small and could hardly accommodate the twenty men and ten women that were sometimes there. The sheikh concluded – I'm sorry to say, on the basis of some

of my photographs – that there was too little distance between the sexes, and moved the women to the next room. Many of the participants are students, some have a job. There was one Rom from Peja/Peć in Kosovo, Faruk, who said he had belonged to the "Kadiri-Rifa'i" order over there. He lived in a nearby settlement for refugees. In October, 2007 he settled with his family in Canada, where he intended to establish a Sufi circle.

For the ceremony, which lasts about an hour, the men will form a circle, and the women sit in rows. There is extensive Koran reading, mostly Surat Yasin, which is considered to be 'the heart of the Koran,' by Hišam and some brethren; a short sermon by Hišam; and the *zikr* proper. The movement, though executed in a sitting position, is analogous to that in the standing and dancing rituals. The *zikr* starts by seeking God's forgiveness and contains about ten Names, some quite elaborate and some short, like "hayy" and "hu." About one quarter of an hour is devoted to the repetition of "*la ilaha illa Allah.*" There are two or three short chapters from the Koran, some recited a number of times in silence, and special prayers for the Prophet Muhammad as well as for the prophets Adam, Noah, Abraham, Moses and Jesus. There are stages where the Names are ejaculated 'with the heart' that is, unarticulated, and others where the breathing is accelerated to approximately four breaths per second. Both the men and women move to the rhythm, the women in a slightly more subdued manner than most of the men and without making a sound. The ritual ends with a mutual greeting between the leader and the brethren, and with the men shaking hands. There is no music and no instruments are used, but sometimes *ilahis* are sung after the *zikr's* conclusion.

In summer the *zikr* falls between the fourth and the fifth ritual prayer, roughly between nine and half past ten. As of September the *zikr* starts after the fifth prayer. Afterward there is tea and conversation, men and women sitting apart from one another. If someone has made a sacrifice there will be some meat, as well. By midnight everyone goes home.

The singing of *ilahi* hymns – a Turkish custom which may have been borrowed from a Christian sect in Anatolia during the conquest of that region by the Seljuks – can be performed by anyone, but many Sufi communities in the Balkans have a core group who know them by heart or read from printed or handwritten texts. In Bosnia the languages used in the *ilahis* are Turkish and Bosnian; elsewhere, one will also hear them in Albanian or Romany. Sometimes these hymns function as a warming-up to the *zikr*, sometimes they come at the end. They are also sung simultaneously during the *zikr* itself with the Names. The *ilahis* have a role in transferring information, especially to children and aspiring dervishes.

In this order women can be full members. They are sworn in with the same protocol as men, with the difference that there is a male representative who holds the hand of the sheikh, in order to avoid physical contact between a man and a woman.

Hišam efendi maintains that Sufis, including his own community, are ordinary Muslims who engage in voluntary supplementary activities.

Following Nakshbandi orthodoxy, Hišam doesn't give much importance to the saints and to the visiting of their tombs. The saints do have an afterlife, he says, but they can only give *madad*, support of a general nature. The only one who can intercede with God is the Prophet Muhammad. Accordingly, the tomb of Sari Saltuk remains closed but for one day during the year. There is, though, an opening in the entrance door through which anyone wishing to approach the saint can throw some money.

Hišam was my only interlocutor who didn't perceive love as the essential element of the Sufi path. There are other methods, he said, such as *kashf*, the spiritual illumination expounded by Ibn Arabi. In any case, the path starts with *hizmet*, being of service to fellow humans.

***

At the Nakshbandi *tekke* at Kaćuni, which has many more adherents than the Buna one, I attended the sitting *zikr* more than once. The *tekke's* Sheikh, Mesud Hadžimejlić, born in 1937, normally resides in Sarajevo, where he is being treated for the aftereffects of a stroke he suffered in 2003. We will meet up with him again in Chapter Six. In September 2007, Sheikh Mesud had come over for another ceremony in the neighborhood, and he stayed for the *zikr* at the *tekke*. Some fifty dervishes formed a circle, and then the sheikh was brought into the room in his wheelchair, the dervishes getting up and laying their right hand on the heart as a sign of respect. He remained in the chair, which was put in the *mihrab*, which is the sheikh's allotted place, and gave a lengthy speech. Then a lively *zikr* took place, with essentially the same structure as the one described above. After the *zikr* the participants said silent non-synchronized individual prayers for themselves and others of their choice, every time followed by an audible *amin* (amen). At the end there was tea, some meat, and conversation.

It was clear that in spite of the Sheikh's disability, his presence was profoundly meaningful to his dervishes.

***

In Struga, in the south of Macedonia on Lake Ohrid, there is a *tekke* of the Khalwati order called Halveti in the Balkans. They are the most numerous Sufi order in Macedonia. I had visited them in 2004, and Sheikh Arif was kind enough to have me return with my camera in September 2007, during Ramadan. Unlike in Egypt, where the month of Ramadan sees vastly increased *zikr* activity, the sessions in Struga are shortened during that period. However, an additional ceremony is held on Thursday evening. The Thursday *zikr* lasted just over half an hour while the regular one on Friday, after the noon prayer and sermon, took only twenty minutes.

The Struga Khalwatis are intimately integrated with

The Halveti *tekke* in Struga.

the Muslim community at large. The sheikh's son Ilhan, who will take over in due time, is also the *imam* of the mosque in the *tekke*. He leads the regular prayers and delivers the Friday sermon in the three languages every Struga child grows up with: Albanian, Turkish, and Macedonian. Only Romany is absent. After the Friday prayer the dervishes and whoever else is interested stay in the same hall, where the *zikr* starts immediately. After the *zikr* there is coffee, prepared by the old "kahvedži-dede" Džemal, who is also the sheikh's deputy. Lokum, Turkish delight, comes with the coffee to replace the sugar supposed to be lost du-ring the *zikr*, especially when the Name "*hu*" is intoned.

The *zikr* didn't entail an excess of movement. There was an inclination of the head to the right and left and forward and backward, accompanied by a gentle swaying of the body. Only three Names, "*la ilaha illa Allah*," "*hu*" and '*hayy*," were used, but the *ilahis* were exceptionally beautiful. The sheikh told me that a revolving *zikr* had been practiced before but it had not been taken up again when the *tekke* reopened after a prolonged closure. The same applied to the use of musical instruments.

The Macedonian Khalwatis belong to the Hayati branch, introduced in the eighteenth century first in Ohrid, where the founder is buried, and subsequently in Struga, Kičevo, and Štip. The long caps, similar to those of the Mevlevis, worn by the advanced dervishes are typical Hayati garb.

I spent most of the time with Halil Imami, an accoun-tant in Struga who is one of the *tekke*'s dervishes. He told me about the numerous supplementary prayers the dervishes have to perform over and above the five prescribed by the shari'a. Many of these happen during the night and early morning. They can be done at home but Halil prefers the *tekke* and has been issued with a key for that purpose. Apart from that there is the individual homework, called *vazife* here, imposed by the sheikh. Especially, it seems, in "sitting" orders such as this one the dervishes are under continuous pressure to perform their duties. Angels check their efforts, so they believe, but according to the Nakshbandi Sheikh Mesud, there is one compensation: having spent a whole life "under the microscope of the angels," the dervish is spared the examination in the grave that others are subjected to.

All these exercises are meant to take the *nafs*, the ego, through seven stages to a state of perfection, al-*nafs* al-*safiya* or al-*kamila*. The fourth stage, al-nafs al-mutma'inna – the tranquil *nafs*, delivered from all rebelliousness – is that of the advanced dervish, and the remaining stages are the domain of the sheikhs. There are 70,000 veils between man and God, Halil says. At each of the seven stages 10,000 of them are removed. The driving force behind the whole Sufi effort is all-consuming love for God.

Most dervishes inherit their interest in Sufism from their father. It seldom happens that an outsider applies for membership. Women are not admitted as dervishes. All they are allowed to do is watch the *zikr* from the gallery. Though not all Struga dervishes are Turks (Halil, for example, is an Albanian), the lingua franca among them is Turkish. All *ilahis* are sung in that language.

***

The first time I met Sheikh Mehdi, the head of the Rifa'i *tekke* in Rahovec/Orahovac in Kosovo, was in 2002 while visiting his *tekke* with Sheikh Erol from Skopje. Mehdi's father, Sheikh Baki, was still alive. Sheikh Erol had been 'given the hand,' that is made a sheikh, by Sheikh Baki twenty years before. Mehdi served us coffee.

Sheikh Baki died shortly thereafter, and Mehdi, born in 1977, took over as sheikh, taking the hand from Sheikh Mazhar in Gjakova. Then Sheikh Erol died and his son Murtezan, born in 1982, was made a sheikh by Mehdi during the Nevruz festivities at Rahovec in 2006. That was also my second encounter with Mehdi, a sheikh now, who presided over the ceremony. Sheikh Mazhar is only a few years older than Sheikh Mehdi, so there is a whole new generation of Rifa'i sheikhs in this region.

Our third meeting happened when I came by with Sheikh Murtezan in October, 2007. Sheikh Mehdi received us very courteously. He had become a person of authority, much respected by his dervishes, many of whom were appreciably older than he was. There were always a few of them in attendance, sitting silently on the carpeted floor waiting for the sheikh.

We arrived in the afternoon and before long went to the nearby village of Fortesa where the sheikh was to conduct a *tevhid*, a somewhat shortened sitting *zikr*, for the spirit of a female dervish who had died forty days before. Similar ceremonies are held seven days, six months, and one year after someone's death. For non-dervishes, Surat Yasin is recited on such an occasion; for dervishes it is a *tevhid*, centered on the repetition of "*la ilaha illa Allah.*" In return the sheikh is given packages of Marlboro cigarettes and occasionally some money.

The sitting *zikr*, held at the home of the deceased as the custom requires, was attended by some fifty-five men and lasted about an hour. Four Names were used: "*la ilaha illa Allah,*" "*Allah, Allah,*" "*hayy, hayy,*" and "*hu, hu.*" At the beginning and the end special prayers were said for the Prophet Muhammad. One *ilahi* singer accompanied the recitation. The movement consisted of turning the head to the right and the left, sometimes with a slight inclination of the body and a deeper one during the prayers for the Prophet. Since it was Ramadan and the ritual lasted till after sunset a meal was served afterward, and some more *ilahis* were sung. The Rahovec Rifa'is possess a vast repertoire of *ilahi* songs.

This was a *tevhid* with 72,000 Names ("the number of times one breathes – in: *hayy*, out: *hu*- during one day"), that is, since there were fifty-five participants, just over 1,300 per person, or more than three hundred for each of the four Names. The Sheikh counted them on his 500-bead rosary.

The participants, all Albanian, were a mixed company of dervishes and non-dervishes. "How do you know who the dervishes are?" asked Sheikh Mehdi turning toward me. The answer was given by Sheikh Murtezan, who explained that the dervishes are those who don't talk without being given the floor by the sheikh. It is an important sign of good behavior for the dervish never to speak in the sheikh's presence unless the latter addresses him. Since I had briefly done so at the start of the session, I presume that the sheikh wished to gently put me in my place.

Back at the tekke, where we spent the night, Sheikh Mehdi showed us a video of a massive ceremony held there on Muharram 7th, during the ten-day mourning period, the matem, for the Imam Husayn. The seventh is the day the sheikh gives the dervishes some milk and honey, as Husayn gave his seventy-two fellow fighters at Kerbela before they were all killed by the enemy. During the matem the sheikh represents Husayn and therefore wears a red taj instead of the customary white one; red being the Imam's color during his life, black after his death. He takes his milk and honey on the tenth, Ashura, the day of Husayn's martyrdom.

The matem is a time of rigorous fasting. All restaurants in Rahovec are closed. A black cloth hangs over the mihrab in the tekke's zikr room. The sheikh doesn't leave the tekke until after Ashura. Even then, the dervishes go on fasting and mourning for the rest of the month. The importance given to the commemoration of Husayn forms one of the similarities between the customs of the Balkan Sufis and the Shi'a.

Sheikh Mehdi occupies a central position in his numerous and well-organized community. He has a full-time job at it, which he takes very seriously. Whenever he is not visiting another tekke – he finds it very important to nurture and expand his contacts – he is available to his dervishes at the tekke; every morning as of five o'clock (six during Ramadan) until midday, and again from two or three into the night, following his father's example.

The motive for the arduous endeavor to educate the ego, taking it to perfection through its seven stages, is, again, love; being in love with God, as the sheikh put it.

Women are admitted into the order, but not at quite the same level as the men. They are not sworn in with the same ritual, and they mostly sit with the sheikh's mother, or with his wife if the sheikh is an older person. The zikr is held on Friday immediately after the midday prayer and on Sunday evening.

The Kosovo Rifa'is really fit the category of Sufis with the 'iron faith' described in the next chapter, as do their brothers in Skopje who appear in God's Lovers. During the zikr they regularly pierce their cheeks and other parts of the body with iron pins without any blood flowing. On certain occasions the sheikh will stand on a sword placed on the stomach of one of the dervishes. But since in the present photos they are performing a sitting ritual I have included them in the 'sitting' chapter.

Sheikh Mehdi stands on a sword placed on the stomach of one of his
dervishes during a Nevruz ceremony.

Tevhid session at Fortesa near Rahovec/Orahovac, Kosovo, for the soul of a dervish deceased forty days before.

The man to the right with the rosary is Sheikh Mehdi, the head of the Rifa'i *tekke* at Orahovac. Sitting to his left is the visiting Sheikh Murtezan from Skopje. Opposite is the main *ilahi* singer.

The white felt caps are part of the Albanian national dress and not indicative of membership in a Sufi order.

Prayers for the Prophet that conclude the *zikr*. The boy in the green
T-shirt is Sheikh Mehdi's son and prospective successor.

Zikr session on a Thursday evening during Ramadan at the Halveti *tekke* in Struga, Macedonia. These ceremonies are held in the mosque belonging to the *tekke*. This *zikr* lasted for about half an hour. Women are watching.

After the *zikr* coffee is served, prepared by the "kahvedži-dede,"
who is in his eighties.

Regular *zikr* session at the Nakshbandi *tekke* at Kaćuni, Bosnia. The *zikr* is as usual directed by the *tekke's vekil*, Dr. Ćazim. On his right sits his brother Abdusamed, who acts as the *vekil's* assistant in running the *tekke*.

This silver sanctuary lamp, donated by the disabled head of the synagogue...

Individual prayers at the end of the *zikr*.

The Nakshbandi *tekke* on the Buna, Herzegovina. The *zikr* ceremony is held twice a week in the upper story of the *tekke*.

The sessions start with Koran
reading by the *vekil*, Hišam efendi
Hafizović.

Listening to the reading.

After a while the participants begin to move to the rhythm.

Faruk was initiated in Kosovo
into the Rifa'i order and
remained more exuberant in
his movement than the other
dervishes.

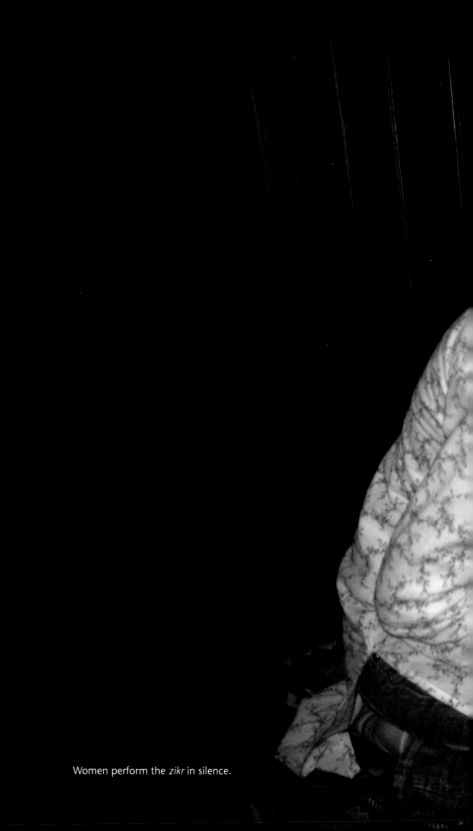

Women perform the *zikr* in silence.

After the session the men shake hands, and sometimes sing *ilahi*s.

The Naksbandi *tekke* at Kaćuni, Bosnia.

6 Standing with God (Bosnia and Herzegovina)

During spring and summer Bosnian Sufis congregate approximately once a month for a 'dovište.' These are massive festivities, some of which may have a pre-Islamic pedigree as prayer ceremonies for rain, such as those held in other parts of the drought-prone Balkans. The meaning of the Bosnian word *dova* is 'prayer.'

A *dovište*, where a thousand or more dervishes may be present, normally starts after sunset. It goes on well after the last prayer, and more often than not ends at the next day's call to early morning prayer, which in summer falls around 3:30am. The program consists of a long series of Koran recitations, songs about the Prophet, *ilahi* hymns and sermons often delivered by visiting high-ranking clerics who will be sympathetic toward the Sufi orders without normally being members. It provisionally ends with a sitting *zikr* led by a Sufi sheikh. Then there is a protracted pause during which the official guests can retire, after which the *dovište* culminates in a standing *zikr* of one or two hours, in which a hundred or more men participate. Since the Nakshbandis are by far the most numerous in Bosnia, most participants will belong to this order, but any Sufi who feels the urge, and even non-Sufis looking for this form of spiritual experience, may join the circle.

The standing *zikr* starts with one big circle comprising all participants. The leading sheikh is in the middle. The movement of the participants follows the same pattern as in the dancing and sitting modes: an inclination to the right with the upper part of the body, straightening and leaning back somewhat, an inclination to the left, straightening, and back to the right. Accordingly, the Names that are recited have four emphases: "*hayy, hayy, hayy Allah,*" "*Allah hayy al-kayyum,*" "*la ilaha illa Allah,*" "*hu, hu, hu, hu,*" and so on. Some of the participants put the right hand on the heart and keep it there. The leading sheikh goes around the circle proclaiming the Name and setting the rhythm, which can be accentuated with percussion instruments like tambourines and cymbals. As the rhythm accelerates and shorter Names are intoned, the movement may be reduced to bowing and straightening, and sometimes to jumping up and down. *Ilahis* will be sung while the circle repeats the Names. At some stage the sheikh will shout, "With the heart [*kalbom*]!" and then the Name is ejaculated in the form of short grunts or barks; a custom found in Egypt, as well, and commented on by Sheikh Zahir in his interview in Chapter Three. The participants stay in the same spot. The sheikh doesn't take part in the movement, but goes around inside the circle, directing, inspiring, and keeping order.

Toward the end, another sheikh may take over and an inner circle is formed which slowly turns around counter-clockwise, other circles form around it, and the *zikr* comes to a close in a compact form with concentric circles close enough together for the participants to lay their hands on the shoulders of those standing in front of them.

Women do not join the circle but they can participate at a distance, moving to the rhythm in silence.

The first assembly of this kind coincides with Nevruz, the first day of spring, at the Mesudija *tekke* in Kaćuni, near Busovaca in Central Bosnia. The Mesudija is called after Sheikh Mesud Hadžimejlić, who is the head of this Nakshbandi *tekke* and also the chair of the "Tarikatski Centar" in Sarajevo, which co-ordinates the activities of the Bosnian orders under the aegis of the Islamic Communi.

The Mesudija *tekke* occupies the upper floor of a spacious new building, which houses a hospital on the two floors below. The hospital belongs to the *tekke* and offers a mixture of conventional medicine and traditional herbal and Koranic healing.

Hadži Mejli Baba came to Bosnia from Konya in Turkey by the end of the eighteenth century and became sheikh of the *tekke* at Vukeljići in 1854, where he is buried. His descendants, the Hadžimejlići, are very prominent in the Bosnian Nakshbandi order. Over the last one-and-a-half centuries they have produced a considerable number of sheikhs. Many of the *zikrs* at the various dovištes are conducted by a member of the family. Whenever Sheikh Mesud is not in Kaćuni his elder son, Dr. Ćazim Hadžimejlić, is in charge as *vekil*. Dr. Ćazim, born in 1964, is an art historian and a very able calligrapher. He has a doctorate from the University of Istanbul and he is a professor of Islamic art at the University of Sarajevo.

Since 2004 he has been publishing the Sufi magazine *Kelamu'l Šifa* three or four times a year. The magazine contains a wealth of information about Bosnian Sufism past and present and about Islam and Sufism, generally.

He confirmed to me that for him, love for God is the central notion on the Sufi path. Through love the Sufi comes to God, he says. Love carries him to God. Illumination and special knowledge are additional to and proceed from love.

As to the Wahhabi effort to introduce a Saudi-style orthodoxy into the Balkans, Dr. Ćazim feels it has started to evaporate. Their approach is too far removed from the Bosnian tradition and mentality to have a lasting impact.

Not all Nakshbandis agree about the standing *zikr*. According to their rule they are supposed to engage in sitting *zikrs* only, which originally were even performed in silence. On special occasions, though, most sheikhs allow the much more exuberant standing *zikr* to be performed. It is sometimes claimed that this is done to satisfy the young, but I have seen many older dervishes participate with gusto, as well.

Pilgrims on their way to Prusac.

As a legal basis for the standing *zikr*, reference is made to a hadith attributed to Ali, in which the Prophet Muhammad describes his companions as "moving like trees in the wind," which is a fitting image for the movement described.

The Hadžimejlići regularly hold standing zikrs. They also engage occasionally in piercing, like some Rifa'is do, due to Sheikh Mesud being a Rifa'i sheikh as well as a Nakshbandi one. The advantage inherent in ritual flexi-bility has been noted by Said effendi Strik, a Nakshbandi *vekil* in Sarajevo, in *Kelamu'l Šifa* 10/11. In olden times, he says, various Sufi orders were represented in many Bosnian towns. Accordingly, a passionate aspirant could join the Rifa'is; if artistically inclined, he would be at home with the Mevlevis; and a conformist character would become a Nakshbandi. Today outside a very few places with a Kadiri *tekke*, an aspiring dervish has no choice but to join the Nakshbandis, who for that reason have to make an effort to accommodate people with different temperaments.

Even so, some of the stricter Nakshbandis feel that the introduction of more lively movements only diverts the attention from the Names, and speak dismissively of "tchorba Nakshbandism;" tchorba being a thick soup into which any ingredients can be stirred.

After the ceremony at Kaćuni, which has to happen entirely indoors because of the weather in March, there is a *dovište* – the only one in the Herzegovina – at the *tekke* by the source of the Buna near Mostar in May; one in Ključ later in May; the "Ajvatovica" in Prusac near Donji Vakuf end of June; one at Karići in the mountains north of Sarajevo in July; one in Vukeljići near Kaćuni in August; and one at Travnik in September.

The Ajvatovica is organized in the honor of Ajvaz Dede, a saint who lived hundreds of years ago. During a prolonged drought he went to pray high in the mountains for forty days, after which the rock split in two and a stream of water came forth that still sustains the area. On the last Sunday in June a massive noon prayer is held at the source. During the night before and after the usual official program, a standing *zikr* takes place next to the mosque of Hasan Kafi in the town of Prusac. In 2007 it started, led by Sheikh Sirri Hadžimejlić, shortly after midnight. After this and until the morning prayer, Sheikh Halil Brzina conducted a sitting *zikr* in the mosque. During the two days of the Ajvatovica there is a festive atmosphere about the town, which boasts the tomb of Ajvaz Dede, rebuilt along with the mosque after being destroyed by the Serbian besiegers' artillery during the 1992–1995 war. There are stalls selling food, soft drinks, recorded music, religious and non-religious souvenirs, and whatnot. Some of the pilgrims arrive traditionally on horseback, passing through nearby Donji Vakuf where they are welcomed in the afternoon by crowds lining the streets. On the banks of the river Vrbas there is a funfair.

Karići is situated at the end of a narrow dirt road high in the mountains above the town of Breza. It has a longstanding *dovište* tradition connected with the tomb of Hajdar Dede, a saint believed by some to have been the brother of Ajvaz Dede. Compared to the Ajvatovica this is a sober, though well-attended, occasion: purely religious, all-male. In 2007, the ritual started around midnight, and consisted of the usual readings, prayers, songs, and sitting *zikr*. The clerics and sheikhs were seated on the ground behind their microphones in the porch of the little wooden mosque, the audience sat in the steep surrounding meadows. The standing *zikr* was conducted in front of the mosque between 2:15 and 3:15am. There was hardly any light, so the reader will have to do without photos of the event. The leading sheikh was again Sirri Hadžimejlić.

In Vukeljići two saints have their tombs: Husejin Baba and Hadži Mejli Baba. Apart from the serious parking problem inherent in big festivities going on in tiny mountain villages, I will remember Vukeljići first and foremost for the joyous, relaxed and mostly young crowd on the

Jeni Džamija in
Travnik, Bosnia.

only street of the village, which was lined with kebab grills and stalls selling the same items as in Prusac. These people had come up the mountain to have a good time, seemingly without giving too much thought to the religious aspects of occasion.

I arrived around midnight after a five-hour drive from my home in Dalmatia, and at that time a lively sitting Nakshbandi zikr was being conducted in the tekke, the biggest building in the village.

Some ilahi singing and a lengthy song in praise of the Prophet followed, attended by a less numerous audience, and then the tekke filled to capacity for a standing zikr (no photography allowed) according to the Kadiri rule, led by the guest of honor, Sheikh Abdul Kadir from Istanbul. The sheikh, a small man with a big white mustache, moved the congregation to considerable passion. The ritual was the same as in other standing zikrs, apart from the final phase during which the participants were jumping up and down. Somewhat against my custom I was myself one of these participants, the room being packed to such an extent that there was no choice but to move along with the crowd. This didn't do me any harm, but it did make clear to me that some experience is required for a smooth performance of a zikr. At the end people lined up to kiss Sheikh Abdul Kadir's hand and that of the host, Sheikh Husejin Hadžimejlić.

A second standing zikr was then started outside by Dr. Ćazim, and took the time remaining until the call to the morning prayer. This zikr, which took place in a somewhat lower-lying area, was watched by a number of women, who however didn't seem to be engaged in zikr as some had been at Prusac. Both zikrs were accompanied by constant ilahi singing.

The assembly in Travnik, once the capital of Ottoman Bosnia, took place inside Jeni Džamija, a mosque in the center of town surrounded by graveyards, to which a Kadiri tekke is attached. It was a modest affair, held between two and six in the afternoon for a few hundred men, attended by half as many women sitting both in the mosque and in separate rooms. There was singing, praying, and some preaching, and at the end a spirited standing hour-long zikr led by the host, a Kadiri sheikh. It was much like the one in Vukeljići. The sheikh, Ibrahim Alibašić, was extraordinarily kind and welcoming, but he had had a bad experience with photos published in Western Europe some twenty years before and felt he should not allow any photography during the zikr.

At the end, as after other zikrs elsewhere, a number of the participants came to kiss his right hand. As Dr. Ćazim explained to me the next day, hand-kissing is a two-way activity. The dervish expresses his respect and his gratitude for the zikr which the sheikh has conducted, and the sheikh gives him blessing and strength. The latter aspect is why many prefer the palm of the hand to kiss and to touch with their forehead. This is where the energy emanates.

Prusac, the Ajvatovica pilgrimage. Standing *zikr* led by Sheikh Sirri Hadžimejlić
on the lawn adjacent to the mosque, sometime after midnight.

Women performing the *zikr* in silence.

Kaćuni, the Nevruz celebration.
Sheikh Sulejman Suljić from Tuzla was
the first of the sheikhs who took a turn
in leading the *zikr*.

The Sheikh is in his eighties. He fought
with the Partisans in the Second World
War, and spent his working life as a me-
chanic. He is a Nakshbandi sheikh as well
as a Kadiri one, and every week leads two
*zikr*s: Kadiri on Thursday evening and
Nakshbandi on Sunday evening. The sessions are attended by about forty dervishes, mostly women; the women mainly
belonging to the Kadiri order. Most of
the men are Nakshbandi. The sheikh is
married to a member of the Alibašić
family, who are Kadiri sheikhs in Travnik.

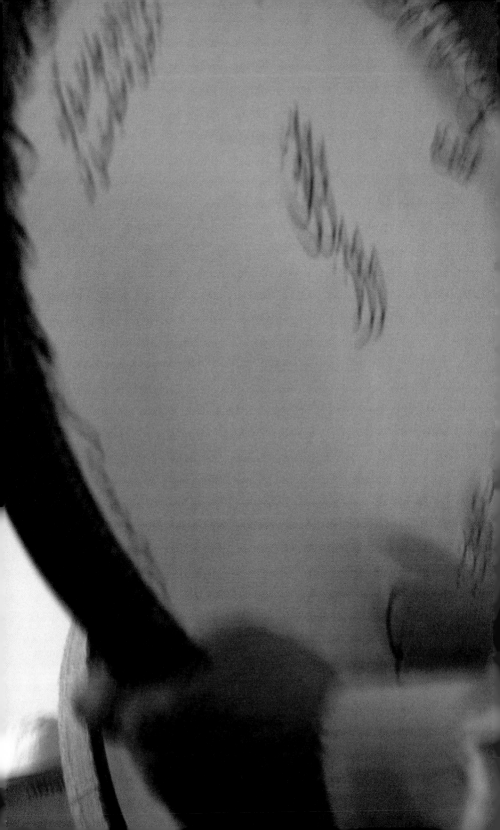

Final stages of the *zikr*, led by Dr Ćazim Hadžimejlić.

Participants line up to kiss the hand of Sheikh
led the *zikr* in Vukeljići .

In the foreground, with a green cap, Sheikh H
the festivity.

Official guests at the Nevruz cremony in Kaćuni.
The Sunni clerics wear their white *ahmedija*s. Among
them are the deputy head of the Islamic Community in
Bosnia and Herzegovina and the mufti of Travnik. They
left before midnight.

The Sufi sheikhs and *vekil*s wear turbans or skullcaps.
Among them is the host, Sheikh Mesud Hadžimejlić;
Sheikh Sirri Hadžimejlić; Sheikh Sulejman Suljić, and the
*vekil*s Mustafa Orman of the Kadiri *tekke* in Sarajevo, and

7   An Iron Faith (Syria)

Issa Touma is a well-known photographer, gallery owner, and organizer of photo festivals in Aleppo. In 2005 he showed me some of his photographs of *ziyaras*, Sufi festivities in northern Syria. The photos were quite impressive, and I gladly accepted his invitation to come and see for myself.

Ziyaras are pilgrimages to holy tombs. They may be pre-Islamic in origin. In the Aleppo area they take place in spring, on dates established following the Christian calendar in its Julian configuration. I duly came over in April, 2006.

On the day of the pilgrimage we left Aleppo early and traveled for two hours in minibuses to the village with the tomb. There we saw some visitors sitting and walking about, but the tomb had been closed for the day by the authorities, who are actively discouraging these festivals, apparently in the mistaken belief that the Sufis are dangerous fanatics. Whereas according to Issa ten or more Sufi groups used to attend only a few years before, no-one seemed to be prepared to take the risk this time around. We stayed for an hour or two and were about to return to the city when a procession arrived of close to a hun-dred Kurds singing and beating drums, and carrying flags, swords, and long iron pins. They said a brief prayer in front of the tomb and then walked on for a few hundred meters, chanting Names and drumming. Then they sat down in a circle with their sheikh on one side and the drummers on the other. For half an hour the chanting and the drumming were kept up.

Almost immediately a man presented himself to the sheikh for a piercing at the waist. The latter established with his fingers how deep he could go without damaging the abdomen and then drove a one-meter long *shish* for half its length through the flesh without any blood flowing. The man walked around the circle with the *shish* in his body for a few minutes and then returned to the sheikh to have it withdrawn.

During the next half-hour this ritual was repeated on another four or five Sufis, and then the ceremony ended as abruptly as it had started, with only a short standing prayer.

As soon as this group had dissolved, another circle formed around an old friend of Issa's, Sheikh Salih from Aleppo. There was the same continuous chanting and drumming, and the waist piercing started right away with a boy, ten years old perhaps, for whom this must have been the first time. He underwent his initiation bravely while relatives stood smiling by, recording the event on their mobile telephones. Sheikh Salih continued with the piercing of another few of his followers, and then bared his stomach, grabbed his scimitar, and pushed it through the frontal part of his belly, not without difficulty and having to lean on the weapon for the final effort. He kept it in for a short while, and then his cousin Sheikh Abu Ali, who acted as his assistant throughout, helped him to pull it out again. His people lit a fire of dry wood and thorns without an apparent purpose. Some moved around but not across it. These included the sheikh's mother, who was the only woman prominently present at the session, though a few women were watching on the sidelines.

One man sat down right in front of me and one by one swallowed the shards of a lamp he had crushed. The sheikh pushed a *shish* into his own right eye socket, which judging by the expression on his face must have been rather painful. There was never any blood visible.

This session, too, dissolved abruptly. There was no opportunity to ask any questions.

A few days later that same week we went to another village at about the same distance from Aleppo. Here we saw bigger crowds watching the entry of the Sufis, of whom there were a number of groups, with their banners, drums, and implements. All I saw them do, however, was pray and wave their flags at the tomb, which was open.

In Aleppo I knew a surgeon who had been a doctor in the Syrian army. He sympathized with the Sufis and visited their celebrations, but was unimpressed by the man eating the glass. From time to time he had seen soldiers desperate for a rest at the military hospital, who had eaten razor blades. Normally, the blades didn't do any damage to the intestine. The main thing was not to eat too many of them over too little time. The same would apply to the consumption of broken glass. Also, he said, the Arabs, Kurds, and Turkmens of the area could endure pain to an extraordinary degree. They visited him with disorders known to be extremely painful hardly uttering a complaint. This made them eminently capable of facing up to ordeals such as these.

This same doctor had another theory. He maintained that the points of the *shishes* were made in such a way that they pried the tissue apart without damage to the blood vessels. According to him this was the reason why there was no blood flowing. He implied that the whole exercise was a gimmick meant to impress the public. I never came across this explanation anywhere else, including Kosovo and Macedonia, where the Rifa'is pierce their cheeks, tongues, eye sockets, waists and throats "when love comes to them," as they put it. They did this without an audience; indeed, there was usually no-one at all watching them from outside their circle.

I saw Sheikh Salih's cousin, Sheikh Abu Ali, briefly

during a subsequent visit to Aleppo. He showed me a
number of scars on his waist, but claimed that there had
been no pain; and, of course, no blood. Apart from *zikrs*
at festivities such as the *ziyara* they assembled once a week,
on the Friday. They engaged in piercing only when they
were overcome by states induced by God: *ahwal rabbaniyya*.
They had to be pure and sincere. All this was done for
the love of God.

Sufis enter the village.

They pray at the holy tomb.

They walk to an open space, drumming and chanting.

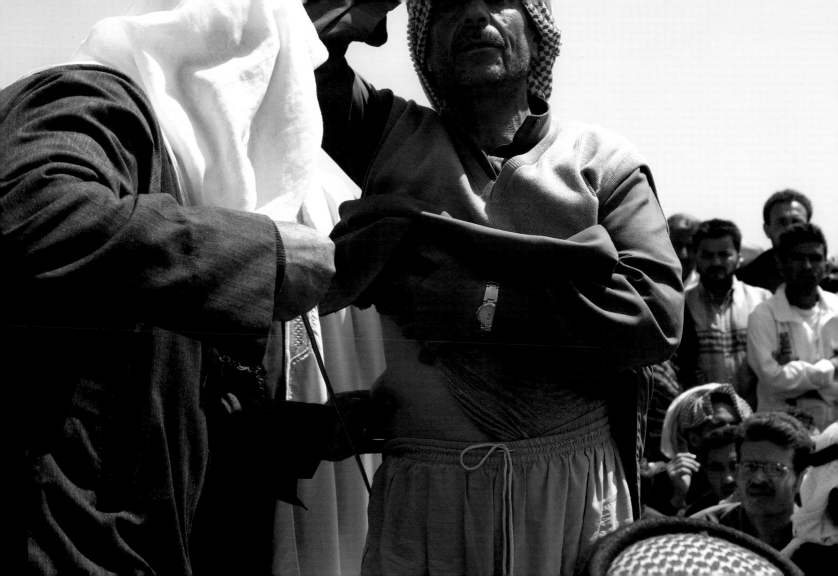

Prayer concluding the session.

The sheikh's mother was conspicuously present at the ceremony.

8 The Prophet's Birthday (Cairo)

The participation of women in mixed *zikrs* used to be customary in certain orders, but these days it is rare, certainly in Egypt. Women do perform the *zikrs*, but usually this happens in a separate place unseen by men.

In 2008 I came across a *zikr* where women were participating alongside men on the birthday of the Prophet, *mawlid al-Nabi*. That year the *mawlid*, which is celebrated on the 12th of the third month of the Muslim year, Rabi' al-Awwal, fell on March 20th of the western calendar. The lively celebration was conducted by the Bayoumiyya order in the open air around 10pm, just outside the side entrance to the mosque of Al-Husayn in central Cairo.

Red is the color of the Bayoumis. The woman with the red scarf made tea for the visitors in addition to her participation in the *zikr*. She told me she was a member of the Bayoumiyya in the Husayniyya, the area to the north of Bab al-Futouh where the tomb of the order's founder finds itself.

Bibliography

Abun-Nasr, Jamil M. *Muslim Communities of Grace: the Sufi Brotherhoods in Islamic Religious Life*. London: C. Hurst & Company, 2007.

Biegman, Nicolaas H. *Egypt: Moulids, Saints, Sufis*. The Hague/London: Gary Schwartz/SDU, Kegan Paul International, 1990.

Biegman, Nicolaas H. *God's Lovers: a Sufi Community in Macedonia*. London: Kegan Paul, 2007.

Bennigsen, Alexandre and S. Enders Wimbush. *Mystics and Commissars: Sufism in the Soviet Union*. London: C. Hurst & Company, 1985.

Cetin, Onder. *Mujahidin in Bosnia: From Ally to Challenger*. In ISIM Review, 21. Leiden: International Institute for the Study of Islam in the Modern World, 2008.

Chittick, William C. *The Sufi Path of Knowledge: Ibn al-'Arabi's Metaphysics of Imagination*. New York: State University of New York Press, 1989.

Chittick, William C. *The Sufi Path of Love: The Spiritual Teachings of Rumi*. New York: State University of New York Press, 1983.

Elezović, Gl. *Derviški Redovi Muslimanski, Tekije u Skoplju*, Skopje: 1925.

Encyclopaedia of Islam. E.J. Brill, Leiden: 1960–2002.

Gaborieau, Marc, Alexandre Popovi and Thierry Zarcone (ed.). *Naqshbandis: cheminements et situation actuelle d'un ordre mystique musulman*. Istanbul, Paris: Editions Isis, 1990.

Halman, Talat (ed.). *Yunus Emre and His Mystical Poetry*. Indiana University Turkish Studies, 1984.

The Holy Qur'an, with Translation and Commentary by A. Yusuf Ali, Dar al-Qiblah, Jeddah.

Johansen, Julian. *Sufism and Islamic Reform in Egypt: the Battle for Islamic Tradition*. Oxford University Press, 1996.

De Jong, Frederick. *The Muslim Minorities in the Balkans on the*

Eve of the Collapse of Communism. Islamic Studies 36:2, 3. Islamabad: 1997.

Frederick de Jong, *Sufi Orders in Ottoman and Post-Ottoman Egypt and the Middle East.* The Isis Press, Istanbul, 2000.

Juynboll, G.H.A. *Encyclopedia of Canonical Hadith.* Brill, Leiden, 2007.

Karamustafa, Ahmet T. *God's Unruly Friends: Dervish Groups in the Islamic Later Middle Period.* Oxford: Oneworld Publications, 2006.

Kelamu'l Šifa, Tarikatski Šasopis. Hastahana Mesudija, 72264 Kaćuni BiH, 2004 ff.

Khalidi, Tarif. *The Muslim Jesus: Sayings and Stories in Islamic Literature.* Cambridge, Massachusetts/London: Harvard University Press, 2001.

Kugle, Scott. *Sufis and Saints' Bodies: Mysticism, Corporeality and Sacred Power in Islam.* Chapell Hill. The University of North Carolina Press, 2007.

Norris, H.T. *Islam in the Balkans.* London: Hurst & Company, 1993.

Popović, Alexandre. *Un ordre de derviches en terre d'Europe: La Rifa'iyya.* Lausanne: Editions l'Age d'Homme, 1993.

Popović, A. and G. Veinstein (ed.). *Les ordres mystiques dans l'Islam.* Paris: Editions de l'Ecole des Hautes Etudes en Sciences Sociales, 1985.

Radtke, Bernd. *Between Projection and Suggestion, Some Considerations Concerning the Study of Sufism.* In *Shi'a Islam, Sects and Sufism* (ed. Frederick de Jong). Utrecht: 1992.

Schimmel, Annemarie. *Mystical Dimensions of Islam.* The University of North Carolina Press, 1975.

Schuon, Frithjof. *Comprendre l'Islam.* Paris: Gallimard, 1961.

Sedgwick, Mark J. *Sufism, The Essentials.* Cairo, New York: The American University in Cairo Press, 2003.

Van Bruinessen, Martin and Julia Day Howell (ed.). *Sufism and the 'Modern' in Islam.* Library of Modern Middle East Studies, v. 67. London: I.B. Tauris, 2007.

Waugh, Earle H. *The Munshidin of Egypt: Their World and Their Song.* The University of South Carolina Press, 1989.

Glossary

Abu Bakr a prominent companion of the Prophet Muhammad and first Caliph

adab (Ar.) good manners, decent behavior

Ahmad al-Rifa'i the founder of the Rifai Sufi order, d. 1182 CE.

ahmedija (Bos., Mac.) a piece of white linen cloth wound around someone's fez; worn by Sunni clerics

Al-Azhar the principal religious university of the Islamic world, centered in the eponymous mosque, founded in 970 CE in Cairo

'Ali the son-in law of the Prophet, fourth Caliph, and first Imam of the Shi'a

Allah God; not specific to Islam; Arabic-speaking Christians say *Allah*, as well

Arif a Khalwati sheikh, head of the *tekke* in Struga, Macedonia

Ashura the festivity on 10 Muharram that marks the death of the Imam Husayn

azan or (Ar.) *adhan* the call to prayer

baba (Tur., Bos., Mac.) a Muslim sheikh or saint

bajraktar (Tur., Pers.) a standard bearer; an assistant to the sheikh of a *tekke*

baraka blessing connected with a saint or a sacred place

Bektashiyya a Sufi order, most prevalent in Albania

Blagaj a town ten kilometers east of Mostar, Herzegovina

Buna a river in Herzegovina, a tributary of the Neretva

Ćazim Hadžimejlić *vekil* of the Nakshbandi *tekke* in Kaćuni, Bosnia

dede (Tur.) a grandfather; in some orders, a fully initiated dervish

dervish (Pers.) *darwesh* a Sufi, a Muslim mystic, an initiated member of a Sufi order

devran (Bos. Mac), Ar.: *dawaran* a rotating mode of the *zikr*

Djakovica see Gjakova

Donji Vakuf a town in central Bosnia

dova (Bos.), Ar.: *du'a* a prayer

dovište an occasion where prayers are offered up

džamija (Bos.,), Ar.: *jami'* a mosque

edeb/edep (Tur., Bos.) see *adab*

effendi/efendija (Tur., Bos.) a gentleman, a title mostly given to religious functionaries

Erol Baba a Rifa'i sheikh, head of the Rifa'i tekke in Skopje until his death in 2005

al-fana' fi-l-ilah (Ar.) disappearing in God, that is, losing one's own self in union with God

Fojnica a town in central Bosnia

Gabriel see Jibril

Gjakova a town in western Kosovo

hadith (Ar.) a tradition about what the Prophet Muhammad said or did

hadra (Ar.) the ceremony of which the *zikr* is the main part

hajderija (Bos.) a sleeveless jacket worn by dervishes in the Balkans

Halil Brzina a Nakshbandi sheikh, head of the Mejtaš *tekke* in Sarajevo

Halil Imami a Khalwati dervish in Struga, Macedonia

Halveti (Tur., Mac.) a member of the Khalwatiyya order

haraka (Ar.) movement

Hasanayn one of the *munshids* of Sheikh Zahir

hayy (Ar.) living; Al-hayy is one of God's Names

Hišam Hafizović *vekil* of the Nakshbandi *tekke* on the Buna

hizb a litany

hodža a teacher of (non-Sufi) Islam

hu (Ar.: *huwa*) He, that is, God

Ibn 'Arabi/Ibn al-'Arabi the 'Greatest Sheikh' of the Muslim mystics and the most prolific of Sufi writers

iftar (Ar.) the meal taken at sunset after a day of fasting during Ramadan

ilahi/ilahija (Ar., Tur., Bos., Mac.) pertaining to God; a hymn

sung by the Sufis of Turkish tradition

imam the leader of the prayers at a mosque; also, one of the twelve Imams, descendants of the Prophet claimed by the Shi'a to be his rightful successors

izun (Bos., Mac.), Ar.: idhn permission, esp., to lead a Sufi circle as sheikh or *vekil*

jeni (Tur.: *yeni*) new

Jibril the Archangel Gabriel, messenger between God and the prophets, who revealed the Koran to Muhammad and made the announcement to the Virgin Mary

Ka'ba the central sanctuary in Mecca

Kaćuni a village in the Travnik area, central Bosnia.

Kadiriyya a Sufi order; see Chapter Two

Kafr Ibrahimi a village in the Egyptian province of **Sharqiyya**, seat of Sheikh Zahir's *saha*

kahvedži (Tur.) a coffeemaker

kalb (Ar.) the heart

kalbom (Bos.) with the heart, that is, unarticulated rendering of the Names

Karbala'/Kerbela a town some 60 kilometers south of Bagdad, where the Prophet's grandson Husayn was killed in 680 CE

kayyum (Ar.) ever living; *Al-kayyum* is one of the Names of God

kashf (Ar.) discovery, unveiling

khafi (Ar.) silent (*zikr*)

Khalwatiyya a Sufi order; see see Chapter Two

Kićevo a town in western Macedonia

kijam (Bos., Mac.), Ar.: *kiyam* a *zikr* in a standing mode

Ključ a town in western Bosnia

la ilaha illa Allah there is no god but God

madad (Ar.) assistance solicited from God, the Prophet and the saints

Matem the ten-day mourning period for the Imam Husayn, culminating on Ashoura

Mawlawiyya a Turkish Sufi order founded by Mawlana Jelal al-Din Rumi, whose members are often called *Mevlevi*, following Turkish usage

mawlid (Ar.) *a 'birthday' festival for the prophet or a saint*

Mazhar a Rifa'i sheikh, head of the *tekke* in Gjakova/ Djakovica, Kosovo

Mehdi a Rifai sheikh, head of the *tekke* in Rahovec/ Orahovac, Kosovo

Mesud Hadžimejlić a Nakshbandi sheikh, head of the *tekke* in Kaćuni

Mevlevi see *Mawlawiyya*

mihrab a niche indicating the direction toward Mecca, to orient the prayer

Mostar the main city of the Herzegovina, situated on the Neretva

moulid (Egyptian coll.) see *mawlid*

mufti an Islamic cleric entitled to interpret the shari'a by issuing *fatwas*

Muharram the first month of the Islamic year

muhibb (Ar.) a lover; an aspirant dervish

munshid (Ar.) a singer at the *zikr*

murid (Ar.) an initiated member of a Sufi order

Murtezan Murteza a Rifai sheikh, head of the *tekke* in Skopje

nafila (Ar.) a pious act performed on a voluntary basis, such as the *zikr*

Naggar one of the munshids of Sheikh Zahir

Nakshbandiyya a Sufi order; see Chapter Two

the Names some of God's ninety-nine 'Most Beautiful Names' and related formulas recited during the *zikr*

nawafil (Ar.) plural of *nafila*

Neretva a river in Herzegovina

Nevruz the beginning of spring, the Persian New Year

Orahovac see Rahovec

Osmani a Sufi healer in Zagreb

Peć/Peja a town in northwestern Kosovo

pir (Pers.) a saint or sheikh

Prizren a town in western Kosovo

Qalaaji, Abdul Fattah an expert on Sufism in Aleppo

Rabi'a al-'Adawiyya a famous female mystic and saint in Basra, d. 801 CE

Rahovec a town in south-central Kosovo

Ramadan the ninth month of the Muslim year, when fasting takes place during the day

rehber (Pers.) a guide, a senior dervish who teaches aspirants

Rifa'iyya / Rufa'iyya the Sufi order founded by Ahmad al-Rifa'i; see Chapter Two

Rumi 'Mawlana' Jalal al-Din Rumi, founder of the Mawlawiyya order and Sufi poet, d. in Konya, Turkey, 1273 CE

saha (Ar.) a court; a Sufi lodge

Sari Saltuk Dede a legendary Turkish warrior-saint in the 13th century CE

sayyida (Ar.) a lady, a female saint

sheikh (Ar.: *shaykh*) a venerable man, esp. a spiritual master, the head of a Sufi community

shi'a a faction or party; the main minority branch within Islam, who recognize only 'Ali and his descendants as the Prophet's rightful successors

shish (Tur.) a spit, an iron pin for piercing parts of the body during the *zikr*

Sidi contraction of *sayyidi*, that is, my lord; used in Egypt before the name of a saint, e.g., Sidi Ahmad al-Rifa'i

Skopje capital of the Republic of Macedonia

Štip a town in central Macedonia

Struga a town on Lake Ohrid in southwestern Macedonia

Sunna custom, esp. that of the Prophet; the majority branch of Islam

Suwa a village in the Egyptian governorate of Sharqiyya

tadž / taj (Pers.) distinctive headgear worn by a sheikh

tarika (Ar.) a path, a Sufi order

tekke (in Bosnia: *tekija*) a Sufi lodge

tevhid (Tur., Bos.); Ar.: *tawhid* affirming the one-ness of God by pronouncing the formula *la ilaha illa Allah*; a ceremony where this Name plays an important role

Travnik a town in central Bosnia

'Umar ibn al-Farid a celebrated Sufi poet in Cairo, d. 1235 CE

vazife, Ar. *vazifa* a duty, a dervish's 'homework'

vekil (Tur., Bos.), Ar.: *wakil* a deputy, esp. a sheikh's deputy

vird (Tur., Bos.), Ar.: *wird* a litany; a dervish's 'homework'

zahir the outer meaning of a text or ritual

Zahir (with a different z) a Rifa'i sheikh, head of the *saha* in Kafr Ibrahim, Egypt

zikr (Ar.: *dhikr*) remembrance; a ritual where some of God's Names are recited

ziyara (Ar.) a visit, esp. a pilgrimage to a saint's tomb

A Roma drummer goes around to announce the end of a
day's fasting at Struga, Macedonia, during Ramadan.